KEWEE R

MW01534204

and the
CRESTVIEW RESORT

Printed in the United States of America
by the
Greenlee Printing Co. of Calumet MI

AUTHOR'S NOTE

The data from which this book was complied were secured through numerous sources. From the many conflicting statements which appeared in the original manuscripts, newspapers and mining reports, this author has chosen the data and incidents which appealed to his reason, after all possible research, as being most accurate. If any errors are detected or important information missing, please contact me. These entries are a combination of many sources, most of which are listed at the end of this compilation.

Sincerely,

Clarence J. Monette
Author

INDEX

The Keweenaw Copper Company was organized in March of 1905 under the laws of the State of Michigan, with an authorized capital stock of $10,000,000, divided into 400,000 shares of a par value of $25.00 per share. The principal purpose of this organization was the development of the copper bearing beds of Keweenaw Point contained in the large land holdings of the Keweenaw Copper Company. They were believed to possess the same elements of value that characterized similar, or identical, beds of copper ore which were being successfully worked in the adjoining County of Houghton by the well-known mines of the Lake Superior district.

In the Report of the operations of the Keweenaw Copper Company during the year 1905, President Charles A. Wright reported that very little work had been done on the copper ore beds on Keweenaw Point, operations having been restricted with one or two exceptions to mining the fissure veins, principally for masses and barrel work which could be treated directly by the smelters without the intermediate process of stamping.

He said that the Keweenaw Point had been without railroad transportation facilities (from Keweenaw County to Calumet and all points south) and that had been the real cause which retarded its development. To supply this deficiency, and to enable it to successfully carry on its plan of development, the Keweenaw Copper Company had acquired the charter

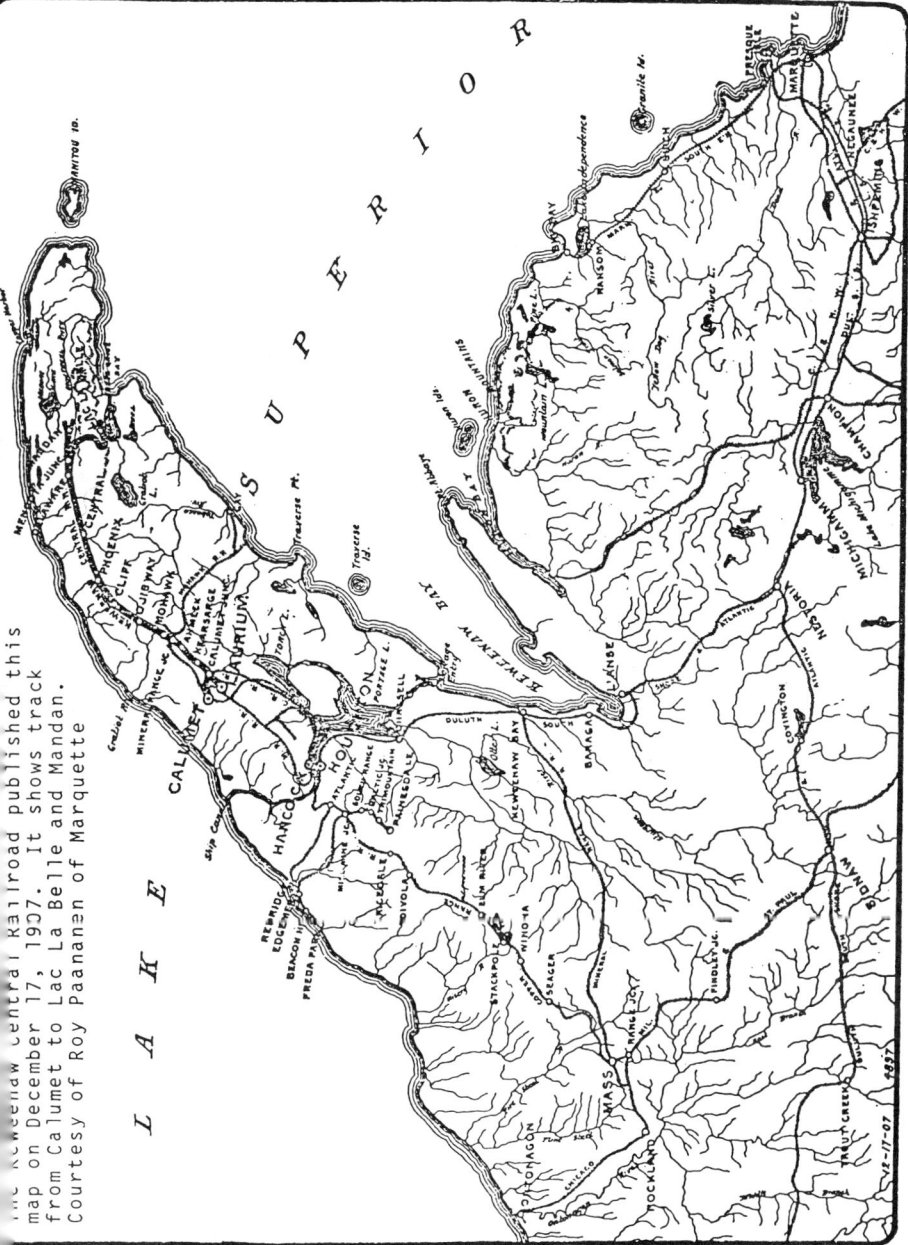

The Keweenaw Central Railroad published this map on December 17, 1907. It shows track from Calumet to Lac La Belle and Mandan. Courtesy of Roy Paananen of Marquette.

and shares of the Lac La Belle and
Calumet Railroad Company. This Company
had some twenty years before, built a
narrow-gauge railroad line from Lac La
Belle to the Delaware Mine, a distance
of about seven and one-half miles, with
the rights to extend the same southwest
about twenty-three miles to Calumet.
The name of this Company was changed to
the Keweenaw Central Railroad Company.

The new railroad company wanted to
operate the route from Calumet to
Copper Harbor, and a map printed in
1906 shows the tentative route going to
the tip of Keweenaw Point.

Many years before the Keweenaw
Copper Company incorporated, in 1865, a
group of investors organized to build a
railroad line from the Cliff Mine along
the range to Lac La Belle. The 38th
Congress issued a Resolution of The
Legislature of Michigan in favor of a
grant of land to aid in the planned
construction of this railroad from Lac
La Belle to the Cliff Mine in Keweenaw
County, thence along the mineral range
to some point on the Montreal River.
On February 9, 1865, it was referred to
the Committee on Public Lands and
ordered to be printed. This is the
railroad of which The Keweenaw Central
Railroad Company now owned the assets
and liabilities.

This first railroad, organized by
the Mendota Mining Company of Lake
Superior, and later known as the the
Lac La Belle and Calumet Railroad,
started actual construction late during
the 1882 season in connection with both
the railroad and the erection of a new

stamp mill at Lac La Belle. The
Mendota Mine was connected with the
Delaware and Clark Mining Companies,
north of Lac La Belle, and consisted of
11,000 acres of property. They started
mining in 1855. The line of railroad
from the rock house at the Mendota Mine
to the mill at Lac La Belle through
Mendota property had been established,
a distance of six and three-quarter
miles. It was not an easy grade as it
had a serious curve at the horseshoe
bend curvature in this mountainous
district. The roadway had been cut out
and cleared nearly the whole distance;
about 8,000 yards of earth-work had
been placed in embankment and 450 yards
of rock cut excavated. Test-pits sunk
along the line of road indicated a very
small amount of rock-cutting, thus
materially reducing the cost of
grading.

The mining company's 1883 annual
report stated that the railroad had
secured the right of way and was
looking to possible extensions in the
interest of other mining companies. It
was now organized as a separate company
called the Lac La Belle and Calumet
Railroad Company, the stock of which
was now owned by the Conglomerate
Mining Company.

This report goes on to say that
the road was 7.6 miles long, laid with
fifty pound steel rails and built in a
substantial manner. It had a maximum
gradient of 158 feet per mile, a
maximum curvature of 19 1/2 degrees,
with a three percent grade, and the
elevation of the mine above the lake

was 575 feet. The stamp mill connection at Lac La Belle was made by building a fifty foot high trestle to a rock-bin at the back of the mill.

Their equipment was brought to the Lac La Belle dock by boats traveling the Lake Superior and unloaded at that place. The first equipment consisted of two steam locomotives and cost the company $20,968.41. They also had six platform cars, box cars and twenty-four eight-wheeled copper ore cars. They were housed and serviced in a wood-frame locomotive house, 34 by 60 feet and two turn-tables had also been built.

One of the locomotives, known as number one, was built by the Baldwin Locomotive Works as 2-8-0 Consolidation during May of 1883, under construction number 6749. It was built with 15 by 18 inch cylinders, 36 inch drivers, and weighed in at 48,000 pounds. Its total weight in working order was 56,000 pounds. It also had a boiler pressure of 130 pounds. Prior to the shipment of this engine, it was exhibited at the Chicago Exposition of Railway Appliances, also held during May of 1883. During mid-October of 1888, it was sold to the Mineral Range Railroad where it became engine number five and was named the "Hancock." The reason for the sale is that the engine was not powerful enough to pull cars loaded with copper ore. The Mineral Range sold it to the Edward Hines Lumber Company of Chicago, Illinois during 1902, and in 1913 it was scrapped.

Keweenaw Central Railroad engine No. 102 at the Calumet depot on January 6, 1911. An A. Isler photo.

    Another locomotive was a "Climax,"
an unusual steam locomotive, built in
1897-1899, a Class B, 25 tons. It was
purchased new from the Climax
Locomotive Company, Cory, Pennsylvania.
The Climax type of engine can climb
very steep grades, say 8 to 12 degrees.
A more direct route could then be put
through to the northwest of the stamp
mill, but above the steep part (which
was most of the journey).

    Some arrangements had to be made
for a suitable rail car to accommodate
the employees and others going over the
railroad, both for convenience and to
lessen the risk of accident. So far
there had been no trouble nor serious
delay in operating the road caused by
the heavy fall of snow incident to the
Lake region.

    During 1883 Superintendent C. H.
Palmer Jr. had reported that
considerable work was still necessary
in raising embankments, deepening
ditches and widening cuts. The
widening of cuts was also rendered
necessary for better winter conditions.
Short side tracks were needed at the
mine to connect the road with the rock
house and the compressor boiler
buildings.

    Since all of the fuel for the mine
was delivered by rail, these short
spurs were necessary to avoid extra
handling and teaming. At the wood
yards, for the convenience in loading
cars, side tracks were still required.
For better operation of trains, a side
track at the summit was also necessary.
Very little if any, additional iron had

to be purchased. The cost of side tracks would only be that of grading and laying. The present locomotive and freight car equipment was sufficient for present requirements.

Thus the Lac La Belle and Calumet Railroad ran between the Mendota, Clark and Delaware Mines and the Lake La Belle smelter and docks between 1883 and 1888. At this time the railroad and equipment was worth $146,000.00.

The annual report ending December 31, 1905, reported under the assets section of the Keweenaw Central Company, listed the cost of the rail road as $238,811.92; equipment cost $5,816.56: rails and supplies were entered at $47.211.63. Part of the railroad company was the Mendota Canal which cost $13,731.08; accounts receivable listed $630.52 and the railroad had $47,546.75 in cash.

For this first year, 1905, Charles A. Wright, President of the Superior Trust Company of Hancock, was the President and Treasurer of the Keweenaw Central; Spencer R. Hill of the firm of Richardson, Hill and Company of Boston was Vice President; Thomas Hoatson, Mining Director; Charles A. Wright Jr., Secretary and Assistant Treasurer; with Directors Thomas F. Cole, James Hoatson, Spencer R. Hill, James N. Wright, Michigan Director of the Calumet and Hecla Mining Company, and Charles A. Wright.

The right-of-way for the Keweenaw Central was secure for its entire

proposed length from Lac La Belle and
Copper Harbor to Calumet except that
portion of the survey crossing the
Bigelow holdings at the Cliff Mine.
President Wright visited Boston to
secure this right-of- way, and soon the
grading crew was able to complete their
work before winter began.

The Keweenaw Central Railroad
Company, starting in May of 1905, had
the old Lac La Belle road nearly
rebuilt with the narrow gauge being
widened so that standard gauge trains
could run over the greater part of the
road. Standard gauge was four feet,
eight and one-half inches. They used
sixty pound steel rail. Grading had
been completed on the extension to
Calumet as far south as the Cliff Mine,
and some distance in that property,
leaving about eleven miles of grading
to do in 1906 before reaching Calumet.

J. J. Byers Company was given the
contract in May of 1905 for the
construction of the route and Sonny Jim
Byers and Wick O'Connell did make the
dirt fly, although no one remains in
Keweenawland who can state how speedily
those men and their associates worked.
The Byers purchased a special steam
shovel for the job and thirty-three
cars which would haul the earth removed
to special recesses and ravines along
the route north and east. During July
of 1905 rails were speedily laid on the
portion of the route previously graded,
and considerable attention was given to
the previous roadbed in the Delaware,
Mendota and Lac La Belle areas.

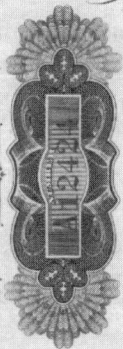

Part of the contract was sub-let to Frank Bushnell, a Houghton contractor who also started to work in May of 1905. It had to be completed by October 1, 1905, with a contract price of $80,000. The new road would go through the locations of Phoenix, Central, Delaware, Madison, Waterbury, Pennsylvania, Mohawk, Amygdaloid, Wyoming (Helltown) and several other small towns along the right-of-way. Mr. Bushnell soon had a force of four hundred men and fifty teams of horses working at clearing the right-of-way and grading the roadbed.

The clearing of the right-of-way was a rather difficult task as the survey ran through deep forests of heavy timber and there was also considerable rock work to be done. Although the rock work could cause considerable delay, Mr. Bushnell was confident that the work would be completed within the time frame.

David Kingston of Copper Harbor, one of the biggest lumbermen in the Copper Country, was able to obtain the rail-tie contract. He had contracts with many of the mining companies, besides furnishing them with underground mine timbers, cutting logs into boards for use in building homes, businesses and surface mining structures.

Grading of a branch line, about three miles in length, through the Resolute, Mandan, and Mendota mining properties now owned by the Keweenaw

Copper Company, had also nearly been finished. The company would soon continue this line in an easterly direction about twelve miles, through the principal lands of the Keweenaw Copper Company, to the mouth of the Little Montreal River, where this company owned a harbor and stamp mill site. It was expected that the line to Calumet would be completed and in operation during the summer of 1906, and that the Keweenaw Central Railroad would furnish Keweenaw County with long-needed railroad facilities. These would rapidly develop its mineral resouces and prove a profitable adjacent to the Keweenaw Copper Company, which owned all of the capital stock of the Keweenaw Central Railroad Company.

The line of the Keweenaw Central Railroad running north from Calumet, where it connected with the Mineral Range and Copper Range Railroads, passed through or close to in the order named the following mining properties: Centennial, South Kearsarge, Wolverine, North Kearsarge, Allouez, Ahmeek, Mohawk, Seneca, Cliff, Phoenix, Frontenac and Manitou, the last which had been organized in the summer of 1905 under the control and management of the Calumet and Hecla Mining Company, its lands adjoining those of the Keweenaw Copper Company.

The Keweenaw Central Railroad Company saw a few changes during its second year, 1906. Charles A. Wright was now the President, while his son Charles A. Wright Jr., took over the

duties of Secretary and Assistant
Treasurer. A new Director, Thomas
Hoatson, was the Second Vice President
and Mining Director. Spencer R. Hill
remained as the Vice President and
Thomas F. Cole was the fifth Director.

The Daily Mining Gazette reported
on April 5, 1906, that an engineering
party in the employ of the Keweenaw
Copper Company was at work in Keweenaw
County, extending a preliminary survey
of the Keweenaw Central to the mouth of
the Montreal River. This would carry
the line twelve miles beyond the
easternmost point reached by the
grading last fall, which was at the
Medora property. The Keweenaw Central
would be extended to the mouth of the
Montreal River this year.

By Sunday, May 27, 1906, the
portion of the grading for one mile on
each side of the Gratiot River had been
sub-let to Robert Hall who already had
a large number of men at work. The
orginal contract for the grading had
been given to J. J. Byers and Company a
long time ago, and part of this
contract was given to Frank Buschell of
Lake Linden, but owing to poor health
he could not continue during 1906, so
it was sub-let to other contractors.

One contractor was working out of
Lac La Belle where they were laying
steel track widening the track to
standard gauge. It was at first
thought that they could not adapt the
first grade laid by engineers up the
steep hill just out of Lac La Belle,

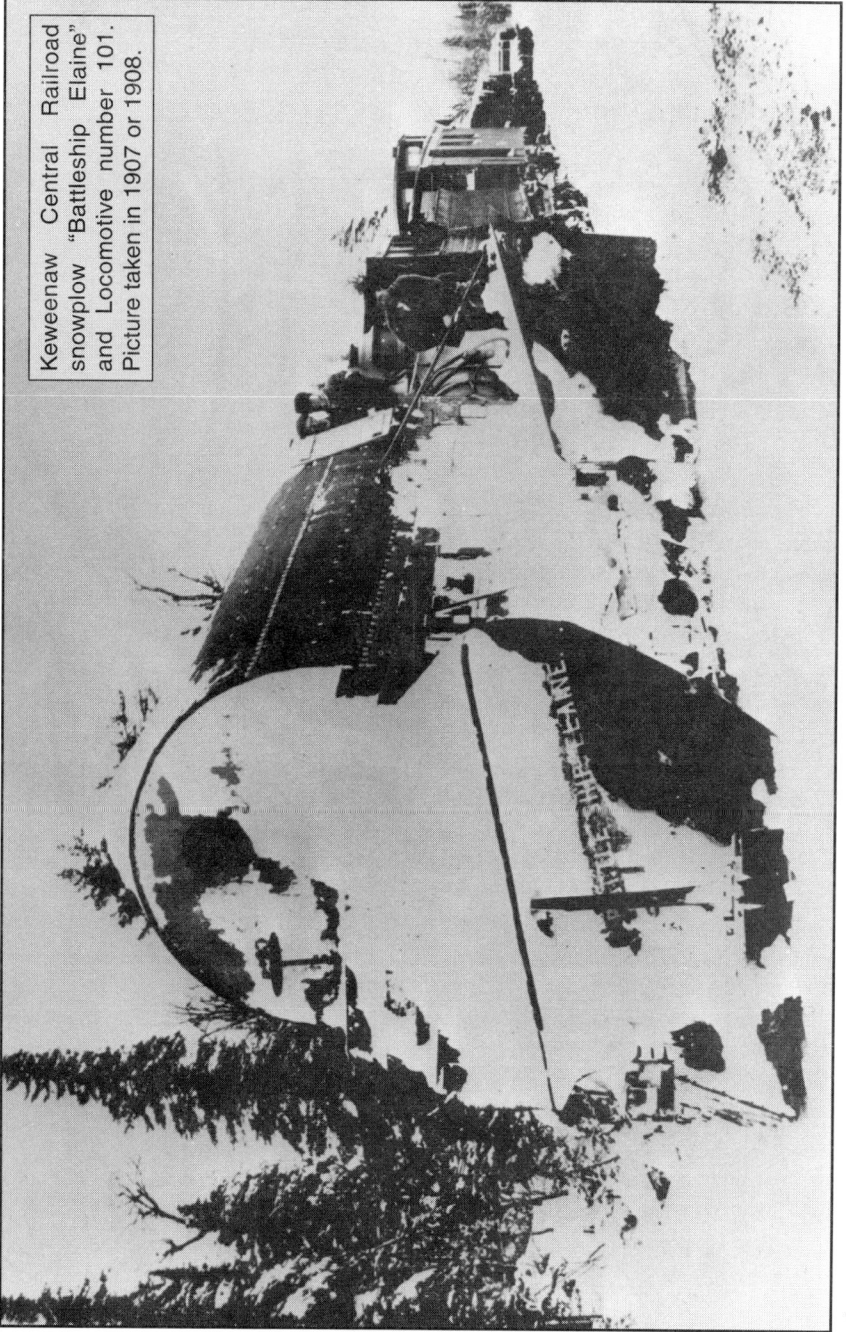

Keweenaw Central Railroad snowplow "Battleship Elaine" and Locomotive number 101. Picture taken in 1907 or 1908.

but as the grade had already been established and some of the rails laid, it was decided to continue instead of taking a more circuitous route where the grade would not be as steep.

On Saturday, November 3, 1906, the Daily Mining Gazette reported that "Today will find the Keweenaw Central tracks all laid between Lac La Belle and Mohawk. While it will take possibly another week before regular traffic can be started, still the management hopes to have a schedule in force by the middle of the month."

"Because of a delay in the receipt of consignment of rail ties the work was delayed for several days, and finally to make the connection of the two ends of the line possible, timber was cut up and used for ties. (It seems that when the supply of ties gave out, the Company sent a gang of men to work hauling logs out of the water at Lac La Belle and cut them up into ties.) Ballasting will be immediately started, and the line made ready for traffic. From Lac La Belle to Delaware the line has all been ballasted, and for a considerable distance south of Delaware."

"It is expected that the first freight shipment over the Keweenaw Central will be early next week. In the early 1880's there were purchased two narrow gauge engines to run on the line between Delaware and Lac La Belle; when operations ceased the engines were stored away, and though in use for only

a little over a year, they remained in
Keweenaw County as a mute reminder of
the explorations of the past."

"These engines have been disposed
of by the Calumet and Hecla Mining
Company, which purchased the property,
and are to be shipped west to be used
once more. These two engines will
probably be the first freight shipment
over the new railroad, and will be
loaded on flat cars, hauled to Mohawk
and then transferred to the Mineral
Range Railroad for disposition further
south."

"Superintendent John Shields of
the Keweenaw Central stated that he
expected that freight shipments over
the line would begin very shortly.
There is a considerable quantity of
material waiting transportation over
the line; the road is promised an
excellent business from the very outset
of its career. Both outgoing and
incoming freight is ready to be carried
over the Keweenaw Central, and the
revenue will be considerable."

"Just when the passenger service
was to start over the Keweenaw Central,
Superintendent Shields was not prepared
to say, but believed that it would be
before the month is over. He said that
it was quite likely that the Keweenaw
Central would secure its own passenger
coaches to operate between Mohawk and
Lac La Belle. Until they arrive it
appeared that the coaches of the
Mineral Range would be used."

"Because of the favorable climatic
conditions for the last two weeks, it

was possible to complete the line a
week earlier than was first intended.
A larger force of men was employed and
by this means operations were more
vigorously pushed. Slight delays in
the arrival of supplies tended to delay
the work, but those were overcome."

The Keweenaw Central had two
locomotives and about twenty cars on
hand and more cars were expected at any
time. These two passenger locomotives
were sold by the Copper Range Railroad
Company to the Keweenaw Central. Named
No. 101 and 102, the engines were of
the 4-4-0 type. Locomotive No. 100 was
of the same type and was sold to a
Keweenaw Central contractor.

Freight was already going over the
line to the Cliff Mine and much copper
ore and other items pertaining to
several mines were coming and going
daily. The Company had just received
notice that one farmer in Keweenaw
County had one hundred tons of hay
which he wanted hauled out as soon as
possible, while numerous contracts for
hauling timber from the Keweenaw County
forests were waiting. Other contracts
for hauling large consignments of
cement and feed as well as mining
equipment and merchandise for various
businesses were in hand. Company
officials said that the prospects were
much better than anyone expected.

The work of laying the tracks from
Lac La Belle to Mohawk was completed
shortly before 2:00 p.m., on Saturday,
November 3, 1906, and the Company had
its trains tied up at Mohawk. Al Lord

1688

KEWEENAW CENTRAL RAILROAD COMPANY.

AGENT'S DRAFT. 1413

NO PROTEST

NO. 365 MOHAWK, MICH., Feb 28. 1917

AT SIGHT PAY TO THE ORDER OF S. F. Steck, Ahmeek, AGENT

Mineral Range RAILROAD COMPANY, $41 52/100

Forty-one & 52/100 DOLLARS

FOR ADVANCED CHARGES DUE THAT COMPANY Frt charges for Feb 1917, a/c

Phoenix Con Copper Co & others AND CHARGE TO ACCOUNT OF

TO TREASURER

KEWEENAW CENTRAL RAILROAD COMPANY

CALUMET, MICH.

A. Jenkins

AGENT

CALUMET STATE BANK,
PAID
MAR 10 1917
CALUMET, MICH.

was the engineer and Superintendent Shields was in charge of the train. The run was made for the purpose of testing the track after the rails had been connected, to make the line complete from Lac La Belle to Mohawk.

Superintendent John C. Shields, as well as other officials of the Keweenaw Central, were present when the work was completed and the trains were given a big reception as they entered the Mohawk location. Every whistle in town was blown for several minutes and the people turned out en masse. No demonstrations had been planned but the occasion would be remembered by all present. The road covered a distance of twenty-six miles from Mohawk to Lac La Belle. Superintendent Shields had taken charge on August 4, 1906 at which time the line went as far as Delaware. The distance from Delaware to Mohawk is twenty-two miles.

The Sunday Mining Gazette of Houghton reported that no attempt would be made to carry passengers for a short time. A great deal of freight that had to be handled would be taken care of now, but arrangements for carrying passengers and giving the people of Keweenaw County first class service would be made soon.

A station, engine shed and supply warehouse had already been built at Mohawk, its southern main operating terminal, and the Company was erecting three more stations at Phoenix, Delaware and Mandan which were along its line. All of the material for

these buildings was there and
construction would be completed in two
weeks. All of these station buildings
were built and framed before they were
received by the Company, being in the
form of portable houses. They were
large, securely built and afforded
excellent accommodations for the
patrons of the Kewewenaw Central
Railroad.

Contractor Byers and Company was
laying rails to the Mandan Mine that
week. This stretch was graded and the
laying of ties and steel was to be soon
completed so that the line to Mandan
could be put into service early in
December. The station at Mandan was
about three miles off the main road and
was connected by a line branching off a
short distance east of Delaware.

Much of the copper ore this
railroad carried came from the shaft of
the Keweenaw Copper Company on the
Medora property. The Mandan shaft was
only a short distance from this shaft.

The railroad company's second
annual report provided the stockholders
on December 31, 1906, stated that "The
Keweenaw Central Railroad Company,
whose Capital Stock amounting to
$500,000 is wholly owned by the
Keweenaw Copper Company, now owns
twenty-six miles of standard gauge
railroad track, partially equipped.
Regular trains have been operating
daily between Mandan and Mohawk, and by
a recent trackage arrangement over the
Mineral Range Railroad, are now running
through to Calumet. The railroad

company at present has no bonded indebtedness. It would probably construct some additional track during the present year and make some necessary additions to its equipment." This report was signed by Thomas Hoatson, Mining Director.

The railroad assets now listed the cost of the road at $434,022.86; equipment $22,860.02; materials and supplies $31,078.82; accounts receivable $1,756.09 and cash on hand at $19,822.40. Their main liability was the capital stock at $500,000.00.

A reporter for the Ironwood Times traveled aboard the Keweenaw Central Railroad during the middle of February 1907, and published an article in his newspaper a few days later, on February 23, 1907. He wrote that "Up in Keweenaw County the casual visitor who may have a bit of sentiment in him rather feels that he is living in the day before yesterday looking at the day after tomorrow. There are villages pathetic in their ruins and there are new mining locations just teeming with progress. The new and the old are everywhere, side by side. It is the recrudescence of Keweenaw County which once was a great mining center, had its day, died, and is revived again."

"A representative of the Mining Journal and another went into Keweenaw County Sunday, February 20, 1907, spent the day there, learned a lot and guessed at more and came back feeling that they had been right on the firing line with pioneers. Keweenaw County's newer history is in the making and it is an interesting process. Contributing largely to this history making is the Keweenaw Central Railroad, which is to be the great artery of the commerce of the county, when that commerce has become the reality which is as yet in prospect."

"The Keweenaw Central has been in operation only a few months, weeks might be better, and it is not equipped with palatial cars, nor has it as yet a roadbed that is free from billows, but "it gets there just the same." The road provides transportation from Calumet to Mandan, the latter being the location of one of the Keweenaw Copper Company's new shafts, the former southern terminus of the road. It runs from Calumet at present over Mineral Range tracks to Mohawk, its own present southern terminus."

"A description of the route of the road in detail would serve no good purpose and it will suffice to say that it follows pretty closely the great greenstone range, a backbone to this great mining district of the Keweenaw Peninsula, which is all of the Michigan Copper Country unless you wish to be arbitrary and claim that Ontonagon County is not part of the peninsula."

"Along the route of the Keweenaw Central are scattered old mining locations, villages built up around the former active mines and abandoned when the workings were given up. The Cliff location is a deserted village. There are no residents there except a few scattered farmers, and the old log houses of other generations are windowless, doorless, broken backed - pictures of senile old age."

"At the Central location things are much the same as the Phoenix, the latest worked of the old mines, and it is gradually assuming the same appearance. The Phoenix was operated up to two years ago, when it was finally abandoned. There is copper there but it costs too much to get it out."

"The trip on Sunday was made only to Delaware, where Delaware Mine Superintendent Penhalegon entertained the visitors and showed them about the location. This mine may be taken as an example of what is being done in various parts of Keweenaw County." The reporter goes on to describe the development of the properties by the Calumet and Hecla Mining Company, and although these far north residents just a few months ago were "living in the woods," with a horse team as their only means of communication with Calumet, which was the base for supplies. Now the Keweenaw Central makes Delaware a suburb of Calumet and the residents there lack no comforts.

"The stay at Delaware was brief, from 11 o'clock and 1:50 p.m., and the visit was necessarily hurried. Then too, snow covered everything and a visit to Keweenaw County for purposes of observation should be delayed until summer."

Harry Reeder waits alone for the Keweenaw Central train at the Delaware depot.

"The Keweenaw Central is the only corporation which can make any use of snow. The road has no snow fences or sheds and as it is treated to blizzards from Lake Superior pretty regularly, some protection must be afforded. Superintendent Shields has solved the problem by building immense snow walls along the track, the snow being merely cut into blocks and piled up as a child would make a snow fort."

"From the line of the Keweenaw Central can be seen a lot of very rugged scenery. It is a very broken country, scarred and seamed with fissures, gulleys, and valleys, but the greenstone range runs along uninterrupted, except for one point where it has a natural break, making possible the road to Eagle River. The latter place is the county seat of Keweenaw County, the residence of Sheriff Bawden. That officer and Prosecuting Attorney Petermann, were at Delaware Sunday, but had nothing to offer."

"As is natural in a new country the sheriff occasionally has something to do. Delaware has a suburb which the miners call Helltown in the village of Wyoming. Here are two saloons, a store and a barber shop or two. Last Saturday was payday and Saturday night was a wild night in Helltown. Sheriff Bawden made his visit to see if anything requiring adjustment by the law had taken place. But for all the celebration there were no serious results. The sheriff has a lot of trouble with "blind pigs," that liquor law which usually follows the pioneer."

The reporter closes with "a day spent along the line of the Keweenaw Central is full of interest and easily conveys an idea of the possibilites which lie ahead of Keweenaw County and its people."

On Wednesday morning, May 1, 1907, the work of ballasting the railroad was started at the north end of the road. An area known as the Mandan swamp was to be taken care of first. A steam shovel was at work daily and a gravel train and crew was engaged in spreading the material. Most of that road had been laid on frozen ground. It was in January 1907 that rails were laid in place, and much snow had already fallen, which made difficult the work of construction.

It was September 2, 1907, that the railroad was inspected and the Commissioner of Railroads and Michigan Railroad Commission issued their report which stated that "The property of this company was inspected September 2, 1907. It consists of the main line from the Mohawk copper mines to Mandan and a branch line from Delaware to Lac La Belle, all in Keweenaw County. This is a new road and was opened for general business about July 1, 1907." (This date is wrong, it was opened in November of 1906 and much work was accomplished after that date.)

"The track in the main line is laid with new sixty-pound steel. Rail joints are fastened with six-bolt angle bars. Ties are cedar and hemlock, about 2,800 to the mile. The road bed is well constructed and fairly well drained. The grades on this line of road are very light (if one can call a three percent grade light) and the alignmnent is good. The bridge structures are in good condition, there being but a few small ones on the main line. The track has little ballast at the time of inspection. The Company was building a track into a rock pile and were about to start ballasting the road with crushed rock."

"The Company is operating four passenger trains a day between Calumet and Mandan. The passenger train service is extended to Calumet over the tracks of the Mineral Range Railroad from the Mohawk mine. It is the intention of the Company to extend their line from its present terminus to Calumet. The map for same has been approved and the right of way secured. The trains are operating under the standard code of rules. Telephones are used in transmitting train orders. No fencing on this line. Highway crossings satisfactory. The Company is building the necessary side tracks."

"The Lac La Belle branch extending from Delaware to Lac La Belle is about six miles long. This piece of road was formerly a narrow gauge road used exclusively for the transportation of copper rock. The Keweenaw Central

bought this property and have re-tied the road with standard ties and changed it from narrow gauge to standard gauge. At present the Company is not operating this branch for a general railroad business, using it only occasionally for excursions to Lac La Belle. It is the intention of the Company to make use of this branch in the near future for general railroad purposes. The rail in this branch is fifty-pound, and the curves are excessive, one of them being twenty-three degrees on a three percent grade. The Company operates this branch, taking every precaution to operate it safely. Motive power and passenger and freight equipment are satisfactory and as required by law. Station buildings are neat and clean."

By Friday, November 1, 1907, the Keweenaw Miner, published in Mohawk, reported that all possible speed was being taken to complete the railroad because of favorable weather the past week or two. Contractor James Byers had about three hundred men employed on the road and sixty-five dump cars and forty teams of horses were also in service. About ten working crews went to make up the numbers.

Beginning a short distance west of the Mohawk depot the road took a southerly direction for a mile or more. Between the county road at Mohawk and the Mineral Range railroad near the No. 5 shaft a heavy fill about twenty-four feet deep and several hundred feet in length was necessary. The Keweenaw Central crossed over the Mineral Range track near this point by means of a long wooden trestle. Three carloads of timber for this trestle had already been delivered.

By a slight descent in grade, the road bed came down to level country to the east of the Ahmeek mine. Passing the Ahmeek a long and gradual curve again carried the road in a westerly direction and to the south of the Allouez mine. After running westward several hundred feet a southerly direction was again taken, gradually making to the east till the Kearsarge mine was reached. Many cuts and fills were necessary between Ahmeek and Kearsarge, most of the work which had already been done. Since Copper City was just getting organized in 1907, the Keweenaw Central was not concerned with this mining location.

At Kearsarge the right of way went through one end of an old burrow pile of poor rock from Nos. 1 and 2 shafts of the North Kearsarge. The highest part of this burrow was at one time seventy feet above the ground. Much was removed, however, and was used for grading by the Keweenaw Central. At the bottom of the pile, ice was discovered which had probably been formed there over twenty years ago.

From Kearsarge the road ran several hundred feet to the east, and then more to the south, with one or two large curves, making toward the Copper Range tracks near the Centennial mine. From Kearsarge to Centennial, three heavy cuts had to be made. One was about 1,600 feet in length, from which the earth was removed to a depth of twenty-eight feet. A second was about 1,200 feet long, and was cut down thirteen feet. A third, about one hundred feet long was also cut down thirteen feet. Another hill several feet in length north of Ahmeek was cut to a depth of seventeen feet.

An article titled "Trestles on The Keweenaw Central Railroad" was printed in the Calumet News, on November 11, 1907. Byers and Company, the Houghton public works contractors, were rushing work on the Keweenaw Central's Mohawk-Calumet extension and were expected to have the grading completed by early December. The work was a seven mile stretch of road bed between Mohawk, the southern terminus of the road and Centennial or Laurium Junction, where the line would join the tracks of the Copper Range, which road the Keweenaw Central would use in running to Calumet.

The Red Jacket depot of the Copper Range would then be the southern terminus of the Keweenaw Central. Company hired men were laying their own steel and the work would be completed in one week.

It was written that "An innovation on steam roads in this district was the use of grade separations at two points, where the Keweenaw Central crossed the Mineral Range spur into Kearsarge. Byers and Company were also building this spur. At North Kearsarge the

Keeweenaw Central tracks would run under
the Mineral Range, the separation being
effected by depressing the Keweenaw
Central track and elevating the Mineral
Range track on a trestle. At Kearsarge
No. 2 the Keweenaw Central track was
run over the Mineral Range."

" Grade separations had not been
used for crossing of steam roads in the
Copper Country except when the Houghton
County Street Car Company used trestles
in getting over the Mineral Range
tracks on its Calumet line. They built
four trestles to make the electric cars
go high in the air in crossing the
steam railroads. The grade separation
was a measure of safety ordered by the
State Railroad Commission and in the
case of the Keweenaw Central and
Mineral Range construction, it was
estimated that it would add $15,000 to
the total cost of the road."

(A special map drawn by Roy
Paananen on January 22, 1990, shows the
Keweenaw Central track going over the
Mineral Range's railroad just east of
Ahmeek; The Keweenaw Central joining
the Copper Range tracks north of Copper
City; the Keweenaw Central tracks going
over the Mineral Range just west of
Copper City; then the Keweenaw Central
going under the Mineral Range's spur
track north of Kearsarge, and then
traveling south to Calumet.)

Company President Charles A.
Wright informed the stockholders of the
Keweenaw Copper Company that their
company had advanced to its subsidiary

corporation, the Keweenaw Central Railroad Company, all of whose capital stock they owned, $121,000.00 for the purpose of completing its railroad and acquiring some necessary rolling stock.

He reminded them that this railroad was an essential part of the development plans of their organization from the beginning, and it was believed would prove a profitable one as well. Without this railroad the transportation of copper rock from the mine to stamp mill and hauling of supplies and construction material for their mines would be attended with such heavy costs as to be practically prohibitive.

Some unavoidable delays had delayed the completion of the line, but before July 1st, 1908, the entire road would be in operation - Mandan to Calumet, 26 miles - Lac La Belle Branch, seven miles - spurs and sidings, two miles - a total trackage of 35 miles, built at a cost of about $20,000.00 per mile. The railroad company operated 26 miles of track in 1907 at a small profit, but would show an increase of business and better results in 1908.

Back at the mine, the Medora Shaft had extensive openings, and while the lode was somewhat narrow, it was well charged with heavy copper deposits. The mine would be in a position to supply several hundred tons of rock daily for stamping about the first of

July 1908 and would be transported over the Keweenaw Central Railroad.

During 1907 the railroad company showed a passenger revenue of $20,319.58; freight revenue of $10,485.98 with other revenue being $1,000.30.

About the middle of April 1908, it was rumored in Calumet that the Keweenaw Central would be running trains into the Copper Range's station in Calumet by the first of June. It was also expected that the work on the right of way would be finished between Mohawk and Calumet by the first of May and that all of the ties and rails would be laid by that time.

Contractor James J. Byers had been making record time in working between Mohawk and Calumet. Considerable rock cutting still had to be done, deep gulleys and ravines filled in, several trestles built and other heavy work accomplished. Work on the line was not fully suspended during the winter months, but additional men had been put on the job that spring.

Work paralleling the line of the Copper Range near the Calumet Junction, Laurium, and Red Jacket, was being done for the Keweenaw Central. Along the right-of-way at this point, timbers had been placed for spanning ditches and ravines and preparations were being made to do grading and filling in, showing that the Keweenaw Central was working almost in Calumet already.

The locations north of Calumet were growing in size daily. Hundreds of people were leaving the Calumet district and were working in Keweenaw County's mines. There was daily traffic between Calumet and the district north that exceeded all expectations entertained by the railroad men a year before, and Calumet businessmen and merchants were doing an excellent business with the communities in Keweenaw County. Besides copper ore and passengers, timber and commodites for businesses and grocery stores were carried. The Bosch Brewing Company of Lake Linden supplied much beer to all points of Keweenaw County using this line. The Bosch Brewing Company even had its own railroad box cars.

By May of 1908 all that remained to be completed was a spur to connect the Phoenix railroad, and the widening of the Phoenix Railroad from a narrow to a standard gauge. Neither of these tasks was a large one; the connection was to be made by June first, according to the newspaper Iron Ore of Ishpeming, written on May 27, 1908.

President Wright informed the stockholders that at the end of 1908 the company had forty miles of track, including sidings, and its equipment consisted of eighty-two freight cars, passenger coaches and four locomotives. He said that the road connected at Calumet with the Copper Range Railroad and was furnishing the necessary transportation facilities for the mining developments of this company and others. The financial statement for

1908 showed the cost of the road at
$704,825.86; equipment at $90,939.95;
material and supplies $4,999.87;
accounts receivable $3,684.32; cash
$18,322.15 and Keweenaw Central
Railroad Company's bonds $500,000.00.

For the year ending December 31,
1908 the passenger revenue was
$25,160.82; freight revenue was
$20,008.08 and other revenue $1,332.39.
Most of their expenses were for
maintenance of way and structures which
cost $7,557.74, and maintenance of
equipment which was $4,225.60.

Company President Charles A.
Wright informed the stockholders in his
1909 annual report that the operations
of the Keweenaw Central Railroad,
resulted in a small deficit for the
calendar year. The reduction in gross
revenue was largely due to the
cessation of mining operations at the
Medora shaft, part of his Company, and
the competition of a parallel street
car railway recently completed between
Calumet and Mohawk.

To offset this loss a recreation
resort was established by the Keweenaw
Central Railroad Company about fifteen
miles north of Calumet, which had a
successful initial season. Increased
revenue from this source was
anticipated, which, together with
expected increased traffic from mining
operations, promised improved results
for 1910. During 1909 six additional
passenger coaches were purchased and
the construction account was increased

by the erection of a casino building at the new resort, "Crestview," a freight warehouse at Mohawk, a section house, additional snow fences and right-of-way fences.

Company President Wright said that "Keweenaw County is a summer resort with many natural attractions, including accessibility, unsurpassed climate, magnificent views, woods, streams, lakes, fish, game, good roads, and is constantly growing in popularity. The Keweenaw Central Railroad is advantageously located to cater to this pleasure travel. It also runs through the heart of the broad mineral belt of this country, much of which is heavily timbered and is said to contain no less than three hundred parallel amygdaloid and conglomerate beds, any one of which may contain copper in paying quantities, and where, adjacent to this railroad, there are now operating a dozen different mining companies. It is confidenty believed that surrounded by these conditions, the Keweenaw Central Railroad will soon develop a profitable business."

During the second week of May, 1909, work started on clearing ground for the extension of the Keweenaw Central Railroad lines from the Phoenix stamp mill to a point near the new Crestview pavilion which was being erected about 1,500 feet north of the mill. The pavilion was 60 by 120 feet in size and was built on a stretch of ground that commanded a magnificent view of Lake Superior. It was built on the highest point of land between the

Keweenaw Central Train 101 at the Phoenix Station on October 13, 1911. Engineer is Stephen Cocking. Courtesy of Michigan Technological University Archives and Copper Country Historic Collections.

mill and Eagle River, just a ten minute
walk to the street that the Keweenaw
County Court House was built on. This
brought it sufficiently close to please
almost everyone in the village, as well
as the patrons of the Keweenaw Central.

The site was very commanding, from
the north or front of the building, as
the ground sloped off gradually for
about twenty feet making a natural and
beautiful terrace. The building was
the only one of its kind in the Copper
Country, being built wholly in the
mission style, and was built by
Contractor Ulseth who was given the
contract and finally received the
necessary lumber and supplies.

This made a new era for Keweenaw
County, as heretofor there had been no
building large enough, or available in
case of damp weather, for a large crowd
to gather. Now the only drawback for
people wishing to visit the beauty
spots of Keweenaw had been removed.
Many people from the Calumet area had
yet to visit Eagle River, the County
seat.

People desiring to go to Eagle
Harbor could depend on securing
comfortable horse-drawn rigs at Eagle
River for a small fee.

The pavilion had a great big
veranda on the north front of the
building, with room for hundreds to
view grand old "Gitche Gumee," made
famous by Longfellow. There was a

kitchen and dining room built so that
the wants of the diner could be
supplied, and also a large dancing
floor, with a dancing surface fifty by
one hundred feet. The Township was
building and widening a narrow path
which was now in use, and was planking
over the damp places so that the
visitors' walk to the village would be
a pleasant one. Good strong wooden
benches were also built here and there
along the path, as ladies with little
ones found them of great convenience.
Being laid out on the flats near the
pavilion was a second baseball diamond,
there already being one which was
formerly used by the Phoenix Ball Club.

The grand opening of the Crestview
took place on Saturday afternoon, June
19, 1909, when Keweenaw's new resort
was thrown open to the public. The
train left Calumet with the Calumet and
Hecla Band on board. The special train
pulled out at 1:40 p.m. and conveyed a
happy bunch of people, who were joined
at stations all along the line with
other pleasure seekers, arriving at the
terminus an hour later. The band
played their fine selections of music
from then until 6 o'clock, with dancing
from 4 p.m., which pleased the crowd.
The round trip rate was fifty cents per
person from Calumet to the Crestview
and return; forty cents from Mohawk.

The next day, Sunday morning, the
train pulled into the Crestview with
two hundred persons aboard, who were
joined by a crowd of between five and
six hundred more, arriving on the train

that had left the metropolis of copperdom at 1:40 p.m. The crowd certainly enjoyed themselves, since numerous compliments on the excellent dancing floor within the pavilion were heard. Hundreds found their way to the lake shore at Eagle River, where some spent the day, while still others went back to enjoy the music by the Tamarack band, which furnished the music for the afternoon crowd. A well stocked lunch and refreshment counter had been installed at the pavilion, where the best of food could be had at all times.

While nearly everyone was enjoying themselves, they were reminded that there had not been sufficient time to finish the buildings and grounds. It would take several more days. The crowd that Sunday was greater than the management had anticipated, with the result that they ran out of everything in the line of eatables, but they stated that this would never occur again, making sufficient provisions to take care of any size crowd that would go there.

The railroad company had placed Charles Oakes in charge of the building and grounds, and as he was also a Deputy Sheriff, it went without saying that the appointment meant order would be maintained. The management wished to make the resort a place that young people could attend without being bothered by the action of young rowdies. No restriction was placed on legitimate sports or pleasure, but order would be maintained.

The Calumet and Hecla Band, beginning on Monday evening, would go to the park each evening until further notice, leaving after supper on the first train, and returning at about 10:30 p.m. which allowed all devotees a chance to enjoy themselves in a place free from dust and flies, and where the cool lake breezes kept the temperature of the casino down to where it was a pleasure to dance.

Beginning the next Saturday, the Keweenaw Central would run trains out of Calumet five times a day to Crestview and the same number back. This would enable people of Calumet and other towns in Houghton County to live at Eagle River for the summer, while they could return on the late evening train or return early enough in the morning to attend to their business. The railroad company had purchased six coaches, now a total of seven in use, which were able to carry at least 2,500 people a day.

Those who preferred to stay at Eagle River for a few days could stay at one of three hotels, the Eagle River Hotel owned by Henry Petermann, the Eagle Hotel by James Phillips, and the Long Hotel conducted by William Long. The lodgers could have their meals at any of these hotels and would be served promptly.

The Township built a short road between the park and Eagle River over which it was practical to drive light rigs and would shorten the time taken

to walk this distance. The Keweenaw
Central did not want people to go to
the Crestview by auto or by horse and
buggy, as they built this resort to
boost their railroad revenue. A trail
had been cut from the pavilion down to
the west and a bridge was being thrown
across the river, so that people
desiring to visit the cemetery could do
so without going down to the village at
all.

Train specials had started two
weeks before the Crestview opened, to
Lac La Belle. The fare was $1.00 for
the round trip to Calumet. A full line
of lunch meals and refreshments was
offered for sale at Lac La Belle. The
Lac La Belle trains were being
patronized as heavily as they were the
year before, even with the Crestview
casino being opened. The Crestview did
not have a turntable for the engine, it
just backed the short distance of track
to the main line.

The first week of July, just three
weeks after the casino opened, nearly
two thousand people traveled to the
resort on a Monday, even though no
music was furnished that Monday
afternoon. Sunday was a record
breaker. The Eagle River hotel was
swamped with business, and many were
disappointed because they could not get
rooms, and over 250 visitors were
served meals, which were said to be the
finest ever served to people in a
village as small as the county seat
was.

A great number of autoists were going to the casino so they were doing a rousing business in the catering line. A feature of the casino was the serving of coffee and tea with light refreshments to auto parties, and a number of them were using this service. The restaurant in connection with the casino was stocked with everything in its line. The Calumet and Hecla band and the Mohawk Band were now entertaining at the resort.

On Friday, August 13, 1909, the attendance at the Calumet and Hecla Promenade required eight coach loads to take members of their popular organization to the Crestview. Twenty-seven automobiles were also used to take people to the resort. This crowd was the second largest that visited the place that season, there being over eighteen hundred who took the day to visit the resort. The crowd was so large that at about 4 p.m. the refreshment stand was all sold out, although the management had made preparations for a large attendance.

Hundreds who had not paid a visit to the resort previous to then were on hand and were delighted with the pleasant casino, the beautiful grounds, and the conveniences supplied to the patrons in way of restrooms and other necessities. The balloon ascension in the afternoon was witnessed by a crowd estimated at 2,000 people.

On Sunday, September 17, 1909, the Crestview was closed to the public for the season. Music was furnished by the Mohawk Orchestra. Over 50,000 people had visited the place that year. Mr. and Mrs. Charles B. Oakes were commended for the orderly manner in which they had conducted the place.

According to Poor's Manual of Railroads for the period ending June 30, 1909, this railroad's rolling stock consisted of five locomotives, thirteen passenger cars, five box cars, thirty-one flat cars, thirty-five ore cars of twenty-five ton capacity each, ten coal cars and one service car, for a total of ninety-five cars.

Poor's Manual also reported the route as follows: Calumet Junction to Mandan, Michigan, 26.2 miles; Ojibway to Ojibway mine, 1.2 miles; Custiren Junction to Custiren, 1.9 miles; Lac La Belle Junction to Lac La Belle, 6.5 miles, a total of 35.8 miles. Trackage: Copper Range Railroad Calumet Junction to Calumet, 1.7 miles; Calumet Junction to Laurium, 1.6 miles), 3.3 miles - total operated June 30, 1909, 39.1 miles. Sidings etc. owned, 7.2 miles.

As of December 31, 1909, the railroad's assets were - cost of road and equipment, $836,934.73; material and supplies, $5,480.83; accounts receivable, $1,109.10; cash, $7,130.17; and Keweenaw Central Railroad Company's bonds, $500,000.00. This year the passenger revenue was $25,018.43, freight revenue $16,514.84 and other revenue $1,569.17. With expenses totaling $47,985.53, the company had a

$4,883.09 deficit.

Their train mileage was 47,216 passenger miles with 17,957 freight miles and they carried 83,506 passengers.

Cognizant of the fact that Keweenaw Central was a commercial line with standard gauge tracks, Carl W. Brown who fired on the Keweenaw Central recalled connections the road had with the Copper Range and the Mineral Range - South Shore Line. Workers would see Chicago, Milwaukee and St. Paul box cars on the route along with Chicago Northwestern, Pennsylvania, Duluth, South Shore and Atlantic and others which came to the Copper Country.

The year 1910 was a quiet one for the Keweenaw Central Railroad Company; due to the great depression in the copper trade that year development work at the various properties on the line was not pushed as vigorously as had been anticipated, and the earnings of the railroad failed to realize the improvement that was expected the previous year. Greater activities were looked for during 1911. It was understood that Ojibway Mine would soon be in position to begin production. During the past few months a shaft had been started on the Kearsarge lode, just North of Ojibway, on the Cliff property, which was under the Calumet and Hecla Mining Company management. Diamond drill exploration had been undertaken on the Senter-Dupee tract about five miles West of the Keweenaw Copper Company's No. 2 shaft, and on

Mr. Estivant's property about six miles
East of this shaft, all of which tended
to develop business in the territory
served by the Keweenaw Central
Railroad. On December 31, 1910 the
stock of the Keweenaw Central Railroad
Company was $730,000.00.

On Friday, June 11, 1911, the
editor of the Keweenaw Miner published
an article saying that the Keweenaw
Central Railroad was proving itself to
be the popular road that year. Where
business had been universally dull
through the Copper Country, and not up
to the usual standard, the patronage
given the Keweenaw Central was greater
than ever before, as was attested by
the immense crowds who took in the
week-end excursions to the many
beautiful breathing spots in the old
Keweenaw. However, the end-of-the year
annual report did not show this.

The crowds visiting the Casino at
the Crestview the past two Sundays had
taxed the capacity of the rolling stock
to its utmost and the coming Sunday
would undoubtedly see greater crowds
than ever visiting the many points of
interest in the county. As of this
time crowds were going just to gather
wild strawberries, which were at their
best.

The Keweenaw Central management
published a pamphlet titled "Beautiful
Keweenaw," for their patrons' use
during 1911. A copy of this pamphlet
can be seen at the Library Archives,
Michigan Technological University
Library. It is twenty-four pages in

length and told of Keweenaw County and
a trip over the Keweenaw Central going
through and describing the communities
of Cliff Mine, Phoenix Mine, Central
Mine, Calumet, Copper City, Mohawk,
Ojibway, Delaware, Mandan and Lac La
Belle.

The Crestview's section stated
that a no more delightful place for a
Sunday school, lodge or society picnic
or outing could be found in the Copper
Country than "Crestview," the
recreation resort owned by this
railroad and operated for the benefit
of the amusement-loving people of the
Copper Country. This resort was
fifteen miles from Calumet on a branch
line.

The casino was the handsomest, the
most complete and convenient structure
of its kind in the Copper Country and
contained a well-appointed lunch room,
kitchen, refrigerator, elevated
bandstand, a superb dancing floor, 50
by 100 feet, smoking-rooms, toilets and
ladies' retiring-rooms. The perfect
sanitation and pure cold spring water
pumped direct from springs by a Perry
pneumatic system were inviting
advantages. At night the casino was
brilliantly illuminated by gas lamps.
Lunches were sold at all times. The
main dance hall opened upon a wide
deck, which was on the west side and
commanded a magnificent view of Lake
Superior and the endless procession of
steamers which were plying the Great
Lakes.

Leading away from the casino in
all directions were shady lanes and
paths to the river, the beach, the
rocky gorges, the falls, up the cliffs,
or a five-mile tramp around the loop to
Eagle River and return. Lovers of
baseball found one of the best diamonds
in the Copper Country, the field being
entirely sod, as smooth and regular as
a billiard table. An excellent cinder
track was provided for races and a
complete outfit for pole-vaulting,
high-jumping, hurdling and other
athletic sports was ready for use. For
the children, swings and other
amusements were furnished. Picnickers
could find tables and benches
distributed throughout the grounds.

The long sandy beach stretched
away for miles to the north of Eagle
River and appealed to the visitors
affording a continual promenade. The
smooth sand, soft but unyielding
beneath the foot, formed a beautiful
yellow carpet extending out into the
water, where one could wade for a
distance of several hundred yards
without being immersed above the waist.
The water was delightfully warm and
scores of bathers spent the afternoon
plunging around in the surf. Children
could play on the beach with perfect
safety.

Perhaps the most fascinating
feature of the Crestview was the road
from the resort to the County seat of
Eagle River. Winding in and out,
sometimes along the ridge of a hill
with deep shady ravines on either side,

Keweenaw Central Railroad passenger train locomotive number 20 at Copper City.

again through a gully, with gentle
slopes rising, snow-clad, to the
sky-line, the path went through a
paradise for the lover of nature. The
scenery along the path was beautiful
and inspiring and the view which
greeted one at the end of the path,
with the placid waters of Lake
Superior, backed by the outline of Isle
Royale, was a veritable scene from
Fairyland. Horse drawn stages could
also be taken to Eagle River.

In addition to the baseball park,
children's playground, bathing beach,
scenic trails, casino and picnic
grounds, the Crestview band or
orchestra would be in constant
attendance to assist the worshippers at
the shrine of Terpsichore, to enjoy the
excellent dancing floor, and to
entertain patrons with concert music.
Special forms of entertainment would be
provided by the company during the
summer season.

A competent and courteous corps of
employees under the direction of the
park manager were constantly in charge,
thus assuring all visitors the best
possible care and attention. These
watchful attendants were particularly
cautious of the comfort of ladies and
children and were ever on the alert to
cater to their welfare. No intoxicants
or disorderly persons were permitted at
the Crestview.

The Keweenaw Central went to Lac
La Belle where the lover of nature who
enjoyed a quiet day in sylvan paradise,

unsullied by the touch of man and
presenting a grateful diversion from
the scorching heat and dust of the city
streets, was able to gather his family
or party with their lunch baskets and
board for this end of the railroad
trip.

Shortly after a whirl around
Horseshoe Bend just out of Lac La
Belle, the train stopped and
excursionists were given an opportunity
to view the enchanting panorama which
stretched out before them for miles.
Lac La Belle, Deer Lake, Bete Grise Bay
and in the distance the cool, blue haze
of Lake Superior were spread out as
some magnificent creation of an
omnipotent landscape architect.

Ample time was given to enjoy the
scene, after which the train dipped to
the lake. No matter how warm it was in
other places, the cooling breeze from
Lake Superior, wafted with a fragance
of the forest, tempered the atmosphere
and helped to make Lac La Belle the
garden spot of the Upper Peninsula.
Several launches were operated at Lac
La Belle and could be engaged for a
trip on Lake Superior, traveling
through the Mendota ship canal to Bete
Grise Bay, passing the Mendota light to
Lake Superior. One could also go to
the whitefish fishing grounds or many
other interesting points.

An excellent lunch room was
maintained and hotel accommodations
could be had during the summer season.
Camping sites could be selected almost

anywhere around the lake and several vacant houses could be rented.

Another Keweenaw beauty spot which was accessible from Keweenaw Central stations was Gratiot Lake. This beautiful lake was five miles from Central where livery accommodations could be secured, and was the only lake of importance where bass abound. Bete Grise Bay was conspicuously a resort for country homes. A number of handsome summer residences had been built and quiet solitude during the summer was enjoyed by the families - while the fishing and hunting season was enjoyed during the fall and winter. Bete Grise Bay was reached by horse team or launch from Lac La Belle.

The pamphlet noted that the Keweenaw Central pierced a district which could not be excelled for hunting and fishing. Thanks to the efforts of the Copper Country sportsmen, working in conjunction with the Keweenaw Central traffic department, the fishing supply had been wonderfully improved during the past few years by the systematic planting of trout and bass fry.

Brook trout streams could be reached from almost any station along the line. Bass were caught in Gratiot Lake and Lac La Belle. Whitefish, lake trout, pickerel, and pike were found in and around Lac La Belle. Deer abound in profusion anywhere in the Keweenaw County and were exempt from the fatal attacks of the cunning wolf. Partridge, duck and other wild birds were numerous. Excellent camping sites were found at Copper Harbor, Mandan, Lac La Belle, Eagle Harbor, Crestview, Eagle River, Central and many other points. Camping equipment was carried as baggage without extra charge by the Keweenaw Central.

The Crestview reopened for the summer season on Tuesday, May 30, 1911. The management had decided to return to their summer schedule. The place would be open for Decoration day, which would please the thousands of people who used this railroad when they wished to communicate with nature in beautiful Keweenaw County.

The train schedule was practically the same, except that the Lac La Belle trains left Calumet at 8 a.m. instead of 9 a.m. so that fishermen and others who desired to spend the day on their favorite fishing streams could do so.

Steve Cocking was one of the most widely-known locomotive engineers the Keweenaw Central ever had. Cocking also worked with the Quincy and Torch Lake, Isle Royale, Hancock, Calumet and Mineral Range, small Copper Country rail lines. Steve died in April of 1959.

Carl W. Brown also fired on the Keweenaw line and remembered the railroad's final days, and its troubles during its final years.

The editor of the Keweenaw Miner suggested that those who were sick should run down to the casino and play, since their ills were in many cases purely imaginary and all they needed to do was get out into the pure and bracing atmosphere of the lakeshore towns. He also suggested people "run down to the county seat of Keweenaw County, put in a week there, getting up in the morning at four or five o'clock, tramp about for a few miles, go out into the lake for a few miles with the fishermen, and get a proper appetite for breakfast, and if you don't feel like a new being, why, it's up to you to see the undertaker and make a bargain for a coffin, they will probably make special rates if you pay in advance."

"If you have more time at your disposal go down to the other towns, put in a couple of weeks at any of them, breathe the pure ozone which has made Keweenaw famous, take your fill of the nectar of the Gods, or if that does not strike the spot with you, you will probably be able to get something stronger, and it's a ten to one shot that you will make regular trips to Keweenaw as long as you live."

The Casino was closed for the winter on Sunday, September 17, 1911, when the Mohawk Orchestra furnished the music for the occasion and there were many sweet strains to please those who enjoyed the tripping of the light fantastic.

As in so many other years, Friday, November 17, 1911, saw the first big

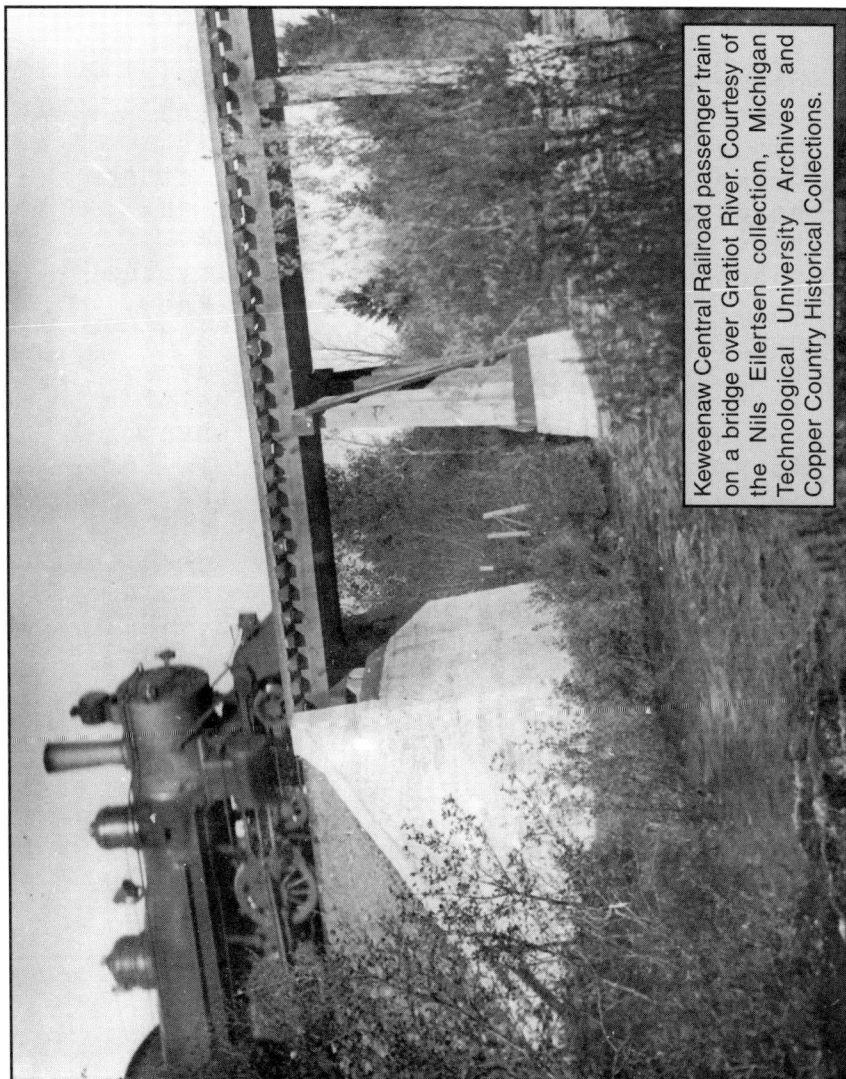

Keweenaw Central Railroad passenger train on a bridge over Gratiot River. Courtesy of the Nils Eilertsen collection, Michigan Technological University Archives and Copper Country Historical Collections.

snow storm of the season, when at least
sixteen inches of snow fell. This fall
of snow made one think of some of the
heavy storms yet to come, many which
were several feet thick. However, the
railroads in the Copper Country were
equipped to take care of just such
occurrences and very little time was
actually lost. The Keweenaw Central
was provided with steel plows which
worked effectively, and like the other
roads up north, very seldom lost any
time by reason of the rails being
blocked. To operate a railroad system
this far north required men who knew
how to tackle the snow problem, and
they quickly learned the work well.
This storm reminded the oldtimers of
the great storm of April 1887, when
four feet of snow fell within
forty-eight hours, and blocked the
roads for several days.

Neither the railroad nor mines did
well during 1911. On November 23, 1911
the Keweenaw Copper Company dismantled
its No. 2 shaft, removing the pumps,
pipes, rails and such. All machinery
was laid up, supplies put away, the
doors and windows of the buildings
boarded up and work at the mine ceased.
Only a small part of the Company's
extensive land holdings of about 20,000
acres had been explored and they hoped
to do better in the future.

The stockholders were asked to
approve the selling of timber on the
lands of the Company. A sale of this
timber to people who would build a
saw-mill at some point on the line of

the railroad would place considerable
money in the treasury and would supply
the railroad with a lucrative business
for many years. With improvement in
the copper trade and greater activities
expected with other properties served
by the Keweenaw Central, the year of
1912 should show an increase over
previous years, according to new
Company President Thomas F. Cole who
had been a director the year before.

For the year ending December 31,
1911, passenger revenue was $19,376.58
and freight revenue was $12,539.25.
While railroad revenue was $33,673.22,
expenses were $48,524.05, leaving a
deficit of $14,850.83.

The Keweenaw Central Railroad
operated at a loss during 1912.
Improvement in its earnings would soon
take place since the stockholders of
the Phoenix Consolidated Copper Company
and the Washington Copper Mining
Company exchanged their shares of stock
for shares of the Keweenaw Copper
Company, on a basis of ten shares of
Phoenix for one share of the Keweenaw,
and twenty shares of Washington for one
share of Keweenaw. The capital stock
was authorized at 400,000 shares at
$25.00 each, or $10,000,000.00. They
issued 209,629 shares at $15.00 paid in
for $3,144,435.00.

The directors also authorized the
selling of the Company's timber. It
was only a question of time as to when
the territory served by the railroad
was opened up and developed so that the

railroad operations could yield a profit according to President Cole. This year the company made $30,555.83 and spent $51,076.51, with a deficit of $20,520.68.

The railroad management announced that beginning with Sunday, January 25, 1913, there would be one train out of Calumet daily, and one out of Mandan also, daily. The change in the running time of the trains was necessitated by the hauling of the logs of Parks and Labby and the Morrison Estate, and with two trains daily the schedule could not be adhered to.

Under the one train each day each way, the schedule could be followed quite well, and this would prove more satisfactory than two trains daily, which could not be depended upon. This service would also be satisfactory to the hunters who would have the greater part of the day to hunt in the woods in the lower end of Keweenaw County.

The Crestview was opened for another season on Sunday, June 8, 1913. Summer had finally arrived and it was announced that the grounds and the casino had been placed in fine condition. Sam Werner, steward of the Laurium Social Club was in charge of the resort. On that Sunday the trains would arrive at Crestview at 8:56 a.m., 2:11 p.m., 7:36 p.m., and 9 p.m., leaving Crestview at 5 a.m., 5:45 p.m. and 9 p.m. Dancing would start when the 2:11 p.m. arrived and would continue until the last train left at 9 p.m.

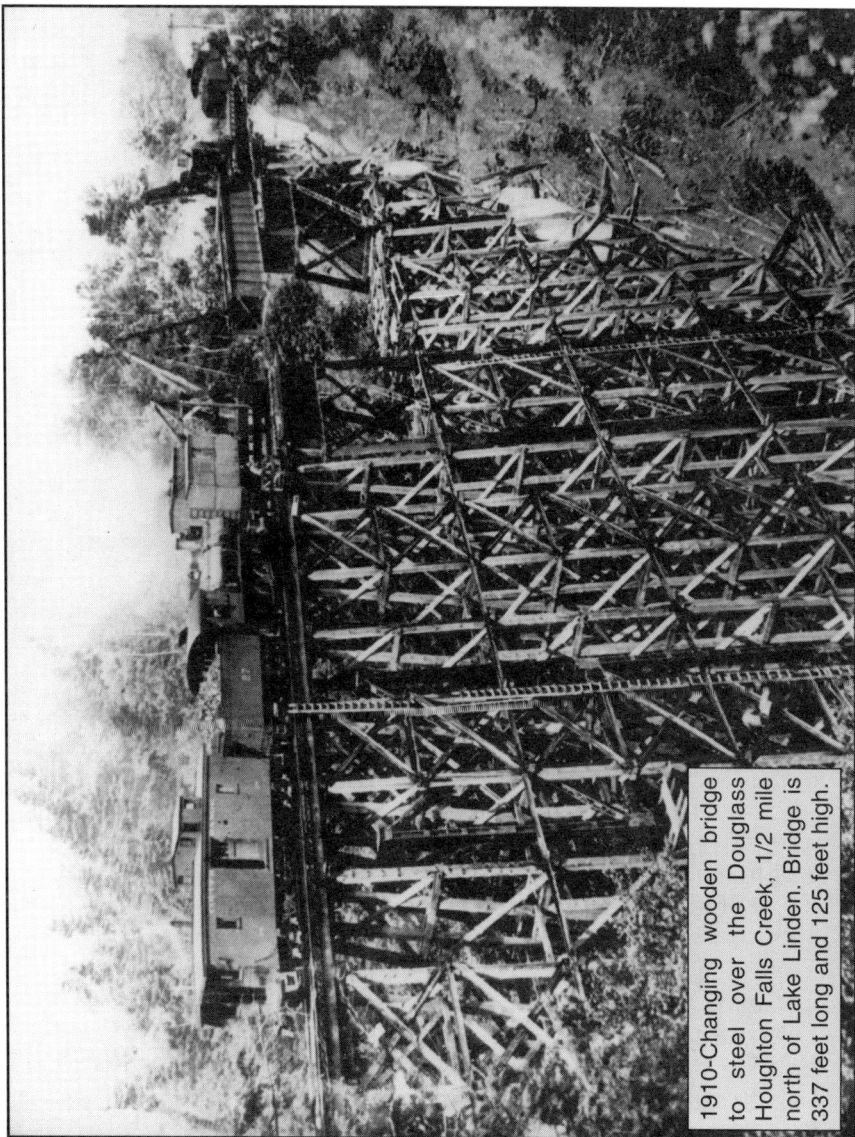

1910-Changing wooden bridge to steel over the Douglass Houghton Falls Creek, 1/2 mile north of Lake Linden. Bridge is 337 feet long and 125 feet high.

For those desiring to spend the day at Crestview and Eagle River, trains would be run down in the mornings of week days, and would also run there in the evenings, but there had to be at least twenty-five round trip tickets from Calumet, or the equivalent, which would be about thirty-five from Mohawk. Many people traveled at this time since the crowds were not as large as they were on Sundays.

Improved service to Lac La Belle began a week later when the Saturday afternoon passenger train out of Calumet leaving at 1:20 p.m. would go to Lac La Belle, so that those desiring to spend more than a day there could be accommodated.

The tracks between Delaware and Lac La Belle had new ties laid throughout the entire length, so that not only the people desiring to go to Lac La Belle, but those who liked to camp at Central and Delaware were pleased during the summer to spend the weekend at any of these places.

During July of 1913, although the weather was anything but great, the gathering of Odd Fellows and Daughters of Rebekah and their friends made the gathering at the Crestview a very large one. The morning was very cold and gloomy, but a few hundred went down on the early trains, and every afternoon train brought several hundred more, so that during the afternoon there were over 1,200 people attending the exercises. The Painesdale and South Range people attending came down in two special coaches of the Copper Range Railroad, which were filled. Others came from Houghton, Hancock, Dollar Bay, Hubbell and Lake Linden. The large crowd was addressed by Grand Master MacNeill and Mr. Rogers who was a Grand Lodge Officer.

Some of their activites were races, tugs-of-war, baseball, and cricket. The Odd Fellows had some copper souvenirs struck for the occasion and they were in great demand. One was a watch fob, with a copper medal, and for the ladies a badge having a copper bar with the word "Souvenir," from which the medal was suspended by a pink satin ribbon edged with green. Manager Werner of the Casino had made arrangments to handle and feed the immense crowd since many did not care about preparing basket lunches. Messrs. Long and Phillips of the Eagle River Hotel also took care of a large crowd of people and their dining rooms were well patronized.

The Keweenaw Miner announced on Friday, August 15, 1913, that the resort was closed a month ahead of time due to the strike that closed all mines in the Copper Country. The Keweenaw Central had felt the effect of the strike so that the management decided to close Crestview for the season. This was sincerely regretted as the place was very popular under the able management of Sam Werner and ·great crowd had been attending every Sunday until the last few weeks.

The Lac La Belle service was, however, continued so those desirous of an outing would take the opportunity of visiting that place. The trains would still go down on Saturday afternoons and on Sunday mornings. Through the week there would be but one train a day down and back which would leave Calumet as usual at 8 a.m. and leave Mandan on the return trip at 3 p.m. On Saturday there were two trains, one leaving Calumet at 8 a.m. and the second at 10 a.m., returning to Calumet at 12:40 p.m.

The railroads' parent company was having many problems due to the strike, as they too had to close their mines. Again this year the railroad was operated at a loss, which was partly due to the industrial conditions which existed in the entire Copper Country. Development and exploratory work was still underway along the line of the railroad and officials stated that they expected increased traffic. For the year ending December 31, 1913 the revenue was $22,957.04 while the expenses were $44,089.70, with a deficit of $21,132.66.

In order to reduce loss of operating the railroad, all work was suspended on December 1, 1913, and the locomotives were repaired during the winter shut-down.

Keweenaw Central Railroad number 20 a 4-6-0, 19x26-57 inch Baldwin. It later went to the Minnesota, Dakota and Western Railroad.

This sudden stoppage caught the postal authorities by ·surprise as they had made no arrangements for the mails to be taken from Mohawk to Phoenix and then to the towns east. The Postmaster at Mohawk wired Washington for instructions and was directed to employ someone to take the mails until the regular contract was let on December 16th. He engaged Parks and Labby to transport the mails and they started a stage line, which left Mohawk every morning except Sunday at nine o'clock. There were nine large sacks of mail in the load leaving Wednesday morning. The mail for Mandan would leave Eagle Harbor twice a week.

The Seventh Annual Report of the Michigan Railroad Commission for the year ending December 31, 1913 showed that the equipment consisted of one passenger and one freight locomotive, (three having been sold as not needed or not having enough power to pull the required number of copper ore cars) five coaches, two combination cars, five boxcars, thirty-one flat cars, ten coal cars, and forty-one cars listed as "all other." They owned 26.40 miles of single track, 9.69 of double track and 2.64 miles of sidings and such. They had trackage rights of 3.30 miles of single track and 3.60 miles of sidings and such. F. W. Taylor was their general freight and general passenger agent.

The year 1914 found the railroad in physically good condition. They had suspended railroad operations on

December 1st the year before.
Operations were resumed on May 1, 1914,
and suspended on November 1, 1914.
This procedure had resulted in a
substantial savings, for there was
little business offered during the
period November 1st to May 1st each
year, and this condition would not
change until a paying copper mine was
in full operation.

During March and April the
locomotives had been thoroughly
overhauled and placed in the finest
condition. In the person of Master
Mechanic Jenkin of the Keweenaw Copper
Company, the railroad company had
secured the ideal man for putting, with
the help of his assistant and engineer
Stephen Cocking, the engines in
excellent shape. The air brake systems
had been gone over thoroughly and
looked as if they just had come out of
the shops. The engines had been
equipped with electric headlights and
everything else done with the idea of
"safety first," always in view.

The general management of the road
was in the hands of William J. Uren,
who was also the General Manager of
both the railroad and mining company.
F. W. Taylor, general freight and
passenger agent, was also the manager
and would look after the business of
the road this year. The office of
general superintendent was abolished.
The road had practically the same train
crew as the past year, with Frank
Chynoweth, Henry Klasner, Stephen
Cocking and August Colleur bringing the
first train out.

Fred Bond at Phoenix, Adam J. Bessalo at Mandan, and Pascal Procissi at Mohawk were in charge of the stations, as they were the year before. A. B. Curtis, who had charge of the Copper City station did not return that year and was replaced by Patrick Harrington who had secured his railroad experience as assistant agent at Laurium and later as operator at the Winona station of the Copper Range Railroad.

Some innovations were started during 1914 in the interest of economy, one of them being that no half fare permits would be granted to the clergy except to those who ministered to the spiritual wants of those residing along the lines of the Keweenaw Central. It was not the intention of the management to refuse the privilege to the regular visiting clergy, such as the Rev. Isaac Wilcox of Mohawk, the Rev. Father Alban of Hecla, or other clergy visiting charges, but the half fare rate would not be granted to those clergymen who merely went down to the Keweenaw on pleasure or hunting trips. A large number of passes which had been granted in the past would be cut off this year.

The Crestview Pavilion was thrown open to the public on Sunday, June 14th. The trains ran the same schedule as the year before and Sam Werner, who had managed the casino in past years, was in charge again this year. The resort was ready for another busy season as many of the businesses in

TOWNS, VILLAGES, HAMLETS AND MINES
SERVED BY THE KEWEENAW CENTRAL RAILROAD

Ahmeek
Allouez
Arnold Mine
Calumet
Calumet Conglomerate
Centennial
Central Mine
Cliff
*Copper City
*Delaware
Frontenac
Gratiot
Kearsarge
Kearsarge Amygdaloid
Lac La Belle
Laurium
Madison
*Mandan
Manitou
Mayflower
Medora
Mendota
Miskwabic
*Mohawk
Montreal Amygdaloid
Ojibway
Old Colony
Osceola Amygdaloid
Pennsylvania
*Phoenix
Resolute
Seneca
Waterbury
Wolverine
Wyoming (with Helltown Location)

*Had a Company built station

Eagle River. With the fishing season opening and the trailing arbutus season opening, Copper Country residents were eager to travel this railroad.

The Daily Mining Journal of Marquette noted that this was Keweenaw County's only railroad and that in accordance with the plan adopted the past year, it would operate only during the summer. Traffic was too light and the cost of operating under snow conditions were too high to permit winter activity. The suspension this year affected a number of lumber operators. Hundreds of hunters took advantage of the last train on Sunday, November 1st, 1914, to get back to Calumet and other Houghton County points from Keweenaw County. The newspaper article further stated that the county was noted for its bird hunting, but the hunters did not care to walk back to their homes, so the Keweenaw Central suspension virtually closed the partridge season in the county.

The Company exercised care to provide fuel and other supplies for the mine development, and northern Keweenaw County merchants placed ample stock of staples in their warehouses before suspension of the train service.

During 1914 their passenger revenue was $8,301.73, freight revenue was $6,330.09 and other revenue was $434.66 for a total of $15,066.48. Since their expenses were $25,712.83,

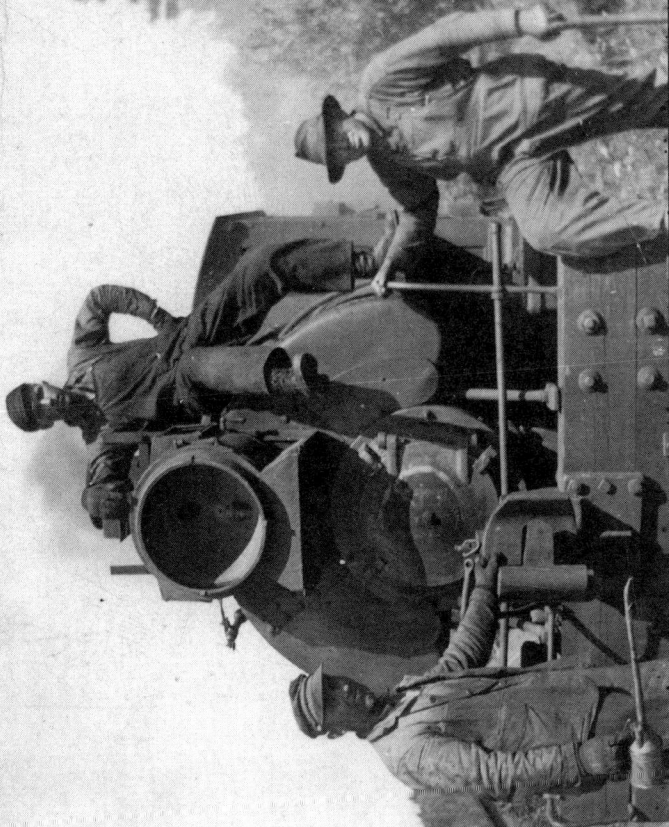

Margaret Hoffenbecker's father with the oil can, brother William on the top, with Jack Wilson on the right. Picture taken in Phoenix.

they had a deficit of $10,646.35 according to F. W. Taylor, Treasurer of the railroad company.

No work had been done on lands of the Keweenaw Copper Company during 1915, since all operations had been suspended. The railroad resumed operations on May 1, 1915 and suspended operations on October 31, 1915. The railroad company's revenue was $15,851.08 with $27,478.66 in expenses, leaving a $11,627.58 deficit.

The Crestview was again opened the first of June and closed on September 25, 1915. The attendance that last day was a record one and the trains were filled to capacity. The orchestra was in attendance and the weather was pleasant. Music was furnished by the "Railroad Four." Again, local lodges and organizations found it an ideal spot to hold their annual outings as well as family picnics. The fare from Calumet to the Crestview, Sunday excursion rate, round trip, was still fifty cents. The fare from Phoenix to the Crestview was only ten cents.

During August of 1915, a first mid-week dancing party was given by the members of the Phoenix Band. A special train left Calumet from the Copper Range Depot at 7:30 p.m. and Mohawk at 7:48 p.m., returning after the party was over, which was about midnight. This year there were large numbers in attendance, and midweek parties were very popular until the close of the season.

The capital stock had not changed for years and the officers remained as T. F. Cole President; Spencer R. Hill, Vice President; Thomas Hoatson as Second Vice President, Charles A. Wright as Secretary and Treasurer and W. J. Uren as General Manager of the Keweenaw Copper Company.

Directors were T. F. Cole and G. G. Hartley from Duluth Minn, Spencer R. Hill from Boston, Massachusetts with Thomas Hoatson, W. J. Uren and Charles A. Wright from Calumet, Michigan. The general office was still in the Calumet State Bank Building in Calumet.

President Cole stated in his Report of Keweenaw Copper Company for the year 1916 that "All work during the year of 1916 was conducted on the property of the Phoenix Consolidated Copper Company." No work had been done at the Meadow Mining Company, Humboldt Copper Company and the Washington Copper Mining Company.

Nothing was said about the railroad. However, the railroad treasurer stated in his report that the passenger revenue was $9,401.00, freight revenue $10,023.46 and other revenue $629.17, for a total of $20,053.63, up from previous years. Expenses were $31,669.79, leaving a deficit of $11,616.16.

During the winter of 1915-1916 the rolling stock had been overhauled and placed in first-class condition. The engines were thoroughly repaired and overhauled and the passenger cars repainted and decorated. Frank Chynoweth had charge of the train and Henry Klasner was his assistant, while Stephen Cocking and August Colleur attended to the locomotive power. Joseph Rom looked after the train at Calumet.

Adam Bessolo had charge of the Mandan station and Anthony Jenkin the Phoenix station. Anthony had an assistant, as he was a pretty busy man this season, owing to the activities about the Phoenix mine. P. J. Harrington had charge of the Mohawk Station and Roy M. Dodge was in charge of the Copper City Station.

According to the Keweenaw Miner, the Crestview opened on June 11, 1916, something that the public had been looking forward to with a great deal of pleasure, when the Keweenaw Central road resumed the usual summer service. The service given was the same as the previous season with three trains to the resort and three returning their passengers. This year the casino was in charge of Joseph Warren and the Ideal Orchestra of Laurium furnished the music. Dance music had always been a feature at the popular playground.

The resort closed on Sunday, September 24, 1916. In his article, the Keweenaw Miner editor stated "The attendance has been so large this year that next season is looked forward to for a still greater attendance. The location of the Casino not being close

Keweenaw Central Railroad locomotive number 29 from the Gregory A. Peet collection.

enough to bother the mining operations of the Keweenaw Copper Company, it is not likely that the resort will be closed next year, if ever, as it has proven to be one of the best drawing cards of the Keweenaw Central Railway."

All of the work for the Keweenaw Copper Company during the year 1917 was again done on the Phoenix Consolidated Copper Company. The investment in the railroad and equipment was still listed at $868,148.93. The passenger revenue of $10,404.84, freight revenue of $10,663.98 and other revenue of $1,834.70 totaled $22.903.52. Since expenses were $33,620.15 a deficit of $10,716.63 was entered in the annual report by F. W. Taylor, railroad company treasurer. The Calumet Junction to Nichols Junction trackage rights were given to the Copper Range Railroad Company during 1917.

The Seneca Mining Company, on October 11, 1917, granted to the Smith and Sparks Company, Houghton contractors, the contract for the construction of a 3,500 foot spur connecting the mine with the Keweenaw Central Railroad, at a point north of the Mohawk train station. The work began the following Monday.

The day the Keweenaw Central ran its last passenger train and had official service on the route was on December 17, 1917. The final train of the Keweenaw Central operated on Christmas Day, December 25, 1917. This

SPECIAL TRAIN SERVICE

TO OLD KEWEENAW

Wednesday, JULY 4th

For an enjoyable outing with the proper environment--spend the day at

Crestview
THE PEOPLES PLAYGROUND

The unrivaled atmosphere of Keweenaw, the enchanting panorama and the sterilized ozone are among the persuading beauties offered recreation seekers by the

Keweenaw Central Railroad

Time of Trains Leaving Calumet,

8:05 A. M. for **CRESTVIEW** and Delaware. Returning to Calumet at 11:30 A. M. This is the big basket picnic train. Get the family together and give them the treat of their lives.

1:40 P. M. for Crestview and Mandan. Returning to Calumet at 6:50 P. M. The Young Folks' train. Take a box of lunch along. Coffee, Ice Cream and Soft drinks on sale at the Casino.

7:00 P. M. for Crestview.

Returning trains leave Crestview at 5:50 P. M. and 9:00 P. M.

Dancing in the Casino
AFTERNOON and EVENING

Refreshments always on Sale at prices that won't stagger you.

Get away from the noise and spend a quiet day at Crestview.

run was merely for historic and clean-up purposes.

After this the Crestview was operated and managed by different private parties but still catered to good crowds. However, this, too came to an abrupt end, as on September 10, 1925, the building caught fire and was completely destroyed. It was a blaze which had no indications of arson. It came through an accident from a "light giving device." Gas lamps were used at night to provide the pavilion with light. At this time the resort was being leased and operated by a private party. Dance music was still being provided by the "Railroad Four."

The "Kay Cee" at one time or other, had seven locomotives, Copper Country railroad historians have said. Numbers 53 and 54 were former Copper Range Railroad 2-6-0 types; Numbers 101 and 102 were "American Type," with 4-4-0 wheel arrangments, likewise acquired from the Copper Range. Number 4 was a 2-6-0 which ended its days on a logging line near Munising; No. 500, a little 0-4-0 "tank engine" (it had no tender behind it) was another busy Keweenaw Central Railroad locomotive. The only engine ordered brand new was Number 20, a 4-6-0 "Ten Wheeler," delivered from the Baldwin Locomotive Works in October of 1908 which saw service until the late 1940's on a Minnosota line, where it was eventually scrapped. Some 95 cars, including about a dozen passenger cars, rounded

The Crestview Park Casino. Courtesy of Sharon Sibilsky of Allouez.

out the equipment roster, all headquartered in the line's shops at Phoenix.

Typical ticketing of the passenger period, from 1907 to 1917, brought riders from South Range to Central for a mere $1.60; from South Range to Copper City for seventy-five cents, and both were round trips.

President T. F. Cole in his Report of the Keweenaw Copper Company for the year 1918 wrote "To the Stockholders of the Keweenaw Copper Company. The equipment owned by the Keweenaw Central Railroad Company had been kept in good condition but much of it was not suited for the heavy duty that later would be imposed whenever rock of merchantable grade was developed and mined in considerable quantities. The sale of this equipment and the rails on the Mandan - Lac La Belle branch was consummated at satisfactory prices. The proceeds had been invested in U.S. Liberty Bonds: $200,000.00 of which is of the First issue and $25,200 of the Fourth issue. These bonds are listed in the financial statement at cost."

The Michigan Railroad Commission's order number 8014 of March 7, 1918, authorized the company to discontinue service and dismantle the road from Lac La Belle to Lac La Belle Junction, a total of 6.50 miles. For several years the company had operated no part of its road during the winter months.

This year the familiar sounds and whistles of the steam locomotives disappeared and with it the rolling

A picnic at the Crestview. Courtesy of the Mac Frimodig collection.

stock of Keweenaw County's only railroad. These are now only sentimental memories of a once romantic age.

Listed in the financial statement under assets were: investment in road $692,345.76; Securities (K.C.R.R. Bonds) $500,000.00; Traffic and Car Service Balances $449.39; Miscellaneous Accounts Receivable $523.35; Unadjusted Claims $155.56; Cash $3,589.50; Profit and Loss $96,258.52 for a total of $1,293,322.08.

Liabilities, according to Treasurer F. W. Taylor, were Capital Stock $400,000.00; Funded Debt $500,000.00; Bills Payable $119,346.40; Keweenaw Copper Company $272,871.81; Audited Vouchers $216.74; and Miscellaneous Accounts Payable $887.13, for a total of $1,293,322.08. Assets and liabilities are the same.

According to Aids, Gifts, Grants and Donations to Railroads including Outline of Developments and Successions (by) Michigan Railroad Commission, Lansing, Michigan and published by the Wyankoop Hallenbeck Crawford Company in 1919, the following is noted:

Amended articles changing names, gauge, etc., from Lac La Belle and Calumet Railroad Company, filed in Michigan, April 27, 1905.

From Lac La Belle to Calumet - 13.30 miles (this is an error)

From Phoenix to Mandan - 13.30
     miles, prior to June 30
     1907

From Lac La Belle Junction, to Lac
     La Belle - 6.50 miles, prior
     to June 30, 1907

From Ojibway to Ojibway Mine - 1.20
     miles, prior to June 30, 1907

From Phoenix to Phoenix Mill -
     1.99 miles, prior to June 30,
     1907. Following 1908 this
     branch is described as the
     Crestview Junction to the
     Crestview Resort. The
     Crestview Junction was 0.50
     miles south of Phoenix.

From Calumet Junction to Mohawk -
     5.80 miles, prior to June 14,
     1908

From Phoenix to Mandan - 13.30
     miles, abandoned on March 7,
     1918

From Lac La Belle Junction to Lac
     La Belle - 6.50 miles,
     abandoned on March 7, 1918.

     Company President Cole had a very
short annual report for 1919, as the
Company did not work on their lands and
the railroad was shut down. Treasurer
F. W. Taylor reported under assets:
invested in road $691,821.07;
securities (K.C.R.R. Bonds)
$500,000.00; Miscellaneous accounts

receivable $401.76; profit and loss
$103,353.51 and cash $2,649.80.

Under liabilities were capital
stock $400,000.00; funded debt
$500,000.00; bills payable $119,346.40;
Keweenaw Copper Company $269,871.81;
miscellaneous accounts payable $544.33
and accrued depreciation $8,463.60.

During 1920 the stockholders were
told "The property has been on a
care-taking basis during the entire
year," and during 1921 and 1922, "No
work was done at the property during
the year." During 1923, 1924, and 1925
the stockholders were told "No work of
exploration or mining was attempted
during the year."

Company President Cole, with his
three Vice Presidents Spencer R. Hill,
Thomas Hoatson and Walter B. Congdon
with Charles A. Wright who was
Secretary and Treasurer, wrote in their
annual report for 1926 that the
"Calumet and Hecla Consolidated Copper
Company became interested in exploring
some of the lands of the Keweenaw
Copper Company which fitted in with
their program of exploration at the Old
Cliff Mine, and in the transportation
facilities provided by the Keweenaw
Central Railroad." The Company
stockholders authorized this.

"At the special meeting of the
stockholders of the Keweenaw Central
Railroad Company (the entire Capital
stock of which is owned by the Keweenaw
Copper Company), held on the same date

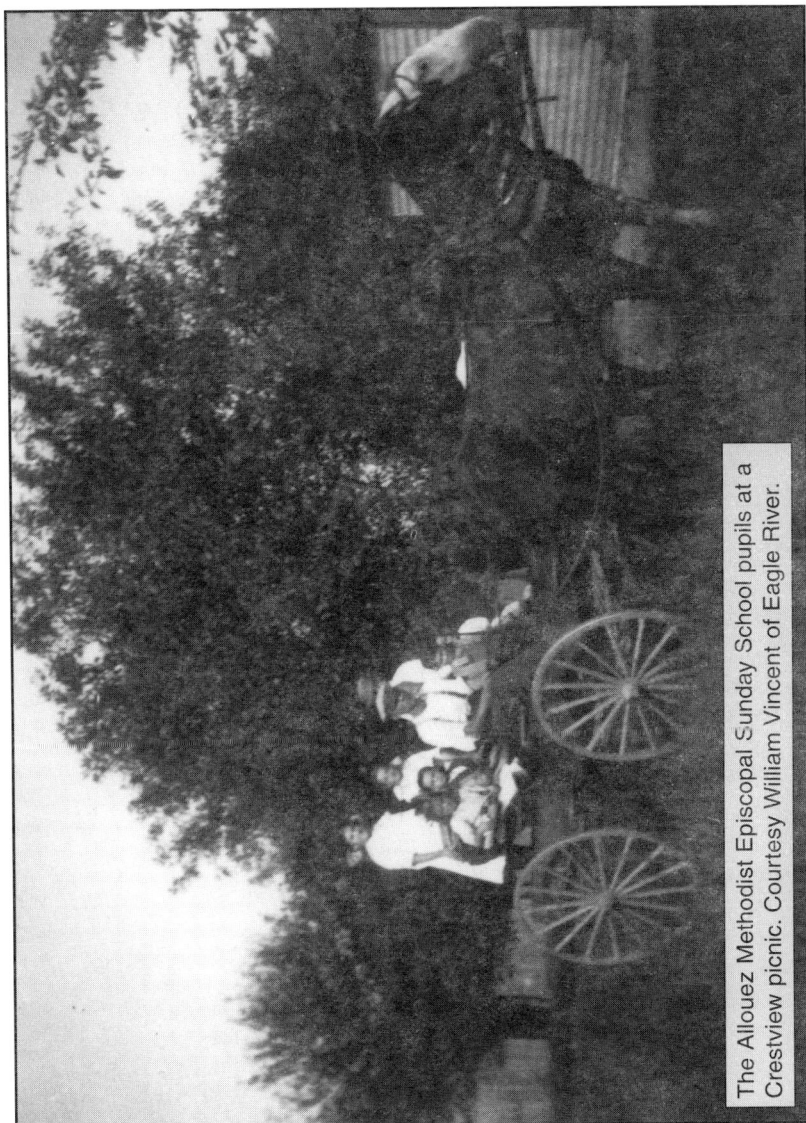

The Allouez Methodist Episcopal Sunday School pupils at a Crestview picnic. Courtesy William Vincent of Eagle River.

(December 21, 1926) authority was likwise voted unamimously to enter into an agreement and to grant an option to the Calumet and Hecla Consolidated Copper Company on all that portion of the railroad lying to the North and East of the Intersection of the railroad with the East and West center line of Section 22, Towhsip 57 N. of Range 32 West. The Keweenaw Central Railroad retains about nine miles of track, of which 8 1/4 miles is main line track from Calumet Junction to East and West center line of Section 22, Township 57 N. of Range 32 West, the starting point of the Calumet and Hecla option. The two agreements and options to the Calumet and Hecla have been executed."

"The Keweenaw Central Railroad Company has granted trackage rights over the remaining nine miles to the Copper Range Railroad Company, which company is thereby enabled to transport over this portion of the Keweenaw Central tracks mine rock and other freight for the Seneca Copper Mining Company; also all freight originating on or destined to points located on the Mohawk and Traverse Bay Railroad owned by the Mohawk Mining Company."

"Both the Calumet and Hecla and Copper Range agreements are reasonable and satisfactory, and assist the progress of mine development in Keweenaw County. They yield additional revenue to the Keweenaw Copper Company and the Keweenaw Central Railroad Company."

The Crestview Resort near Eagle River.

The annual reports for 1927, 1928, 1929, 1930, 1931, and 1932, showed no work done, and the Keweenaw Central Railroad Company financial report was not changed from the reports of years before.

The stockholders received a lengthy annual report for 1933. The Keweenaw Copper Company's address was now 101 Quincy Street, Hancock and they were told "It will be seen from the Balance Sheet of Keweenaw Copper Company that the book value of the lands and the investment in the railroad company have been reduced from cost previously shown, to arbitrary amounts intended to be below ultimate realizable value, which can not now be estimated with an exactness." The main purpose of the letter was to tell the stockholders that the Company was in financial trouble and needed more money through assessments and such. Seems that many of the stockholders had not paid their share of Assessment No. 8. The Company had not paid their taxes for the years 1932 and 1933 and if they were redeemed from a sale held in May of 1936, the title would be lost to the Company.

An entry in the railroad's finance report stated under investment in road "Being the cost of 17 miles of main line and 1.21 miles of side tracks and spurs. Nine miles of tracks are under lease to Copper Range Railroad Company; eight miles of tracks are unleased; and the remainder consists of right-of-way from which rails were taken up in 1918." Their taxes for 1932 and 1933 were $2,440.12. Their only income for 1933 was from the Copper Range Railroad Company's lease for a portion of the road, and that was $1,899.16. Salaries of clerks and attendants was $237.50, while the officers collected $600.00 for their salaries.

During 1932 it was necessary to transfer some rail cars of cement, pavement meshing and rock for road building purposes, to Phoenix. After considering all transit opportunities, it was decided to look over the track, place ties where necessasary and steam up old Locomotive No. 10. The project worked and the necessary materials were moved from Mohawk to Phoenix by the old Keweenaw Central route which had been abandoned. Joseph Hoffenbacker acted as engineer of the locomotive on its last unofficial trip into Keweenaw County.

The typed annual report for 1934 was the second long one to support the Company's financial problems. Walter B. Congdon of Duluth was now the President; Edward C. Congdon of Duluth, Vice President; Robert Congdon of Duluth, Vice President, and Charles A. Wright of Hancock was listed as the Secretary and Treasurer. Other Directors were Harvie A. Garver of Duluth; James Wanless of Duluth and A. L. Warner of Minneapolis, Minn.

The parent company's debts increased and a market value of the

securities owned by the Company
declined. They borrowed another
$37,000.00 from Mr. Edward C. Congdon
bringing its total to $94,000.00. The
official registered office was changed
from Calumet to Hancock and was now 101
Quincy Street, Hancock, Michigan. The
Keweenaw Central's financial page
stayed about the same as in past years.

The Company did not hold a
stockholder's annual meeting in 1935
because there was no business requiring
a meeting and to avoid unnecessary
expenses. However, at a special
meeting of stockholders held on March
9, 1935, the Company's charter was
amended and they reduced the par value
of its shares from $25.00 each to $1.00
each and made all outstanding shares
full-paid and non-assessable. The only
money made during 1935 was through
sales of real-estate and timber
aggregating to $7,000.00.

During this year the Keweenaw
Central Railroad Company's charter was
amended to extend the corporate
existence of that company and to reduce
the par-value of its shares from
$100.00 to $5.00 each. Also during the
year 1935, $500,000.00 face amount of
Keweenaw Central Railroad Company
bonds, held by the Keweenaw Copper
Company as security for the
indebtedness of the railroad company,
were returned to the railroad company
and destroyed, and the mortgage
securing the bonds satisfied. As the
Copper Company owned all the capital
stock of the railroad company, and the

latter had no debts except to the copper company, the possession of the bonds were of no benefit to the copper company. At the end of 1935 the railroad company had $25.51 in cash at the Superior National Bank of Hancock and $150.00 in the Merchants and Miners Bank of Calumet. A frozen deposit of $204.11 was in the Superior National Bank. They were still getting $600.00 per year from the Copper Range Railroad Company for track rental, their only income.

The railroad company did not change much between the years of 1936 and 1942. Their only income in 1942 was the same as in many years, $600.00 from the Copper Range Railroad Company.

In July of 1944, purchase of lands and personal property of the Keweenaw Copper Company by the Calumet and Hecla Consolidated Copper Company was approved at a special meeting of the stockholders by that Company. The purchase included all capital stock of the mine and railroad. The Calumet and Hecla lands adjoined much of the Keweenaw Copper Company. The purchase involved 34,500 acres of land in Keweenaw County and all of the capital stock of the Keweenaw Central Railroad Company, a small part of which had been under lease for the past several years. Some of the best summer resort lands in the Upper Peninsula were included in the property purchased.

The Crestview Resort near Eagle Harbor.

Many years later a legal advertisement appeared in the Daily Mining Gazette and was run on June 2, 9, and 16, 1967. The two by one-and-a-half inch "Notice" was as follows: "Notice is hereby given that the Keweenaw Central Railroad Company, a Michigan corporation, is being dissolved. Any person, firm or corporation having a claim against this company is requested to present his claim at the registered office of the company, 1 Calumet Avenue, Calumet, Michigan, c/o Mr. G. E. Lengyel on or before June 23, 1967, the date fixed for distributing the assets of the company." It was signed by P. G. Meyers, Asst. Secretary on June 2, 1967.

The Keweenaw Central Railroad was born a second time when it organized and operated a Copper Country passenger excursion scenic train from Calumet to Lake Linden from July 1, 1967, through 1971. The Keweenaw Central Railway, formed by four midwestern men, acquired the existing Keweenaw Central trackage from Calumet Junction to Copper City, along with the Copper Range Railroad right of way from the North Sixth Street freighthouse in Calumet to this junction and southward over Bridge No. 30 in Lake Linden. This route would give visitors a fine opportunity to observe the Calumet copper region as well as Lake Linden mill operations.

The officials were President Clinton Jones Jr., formerly of Pewaukee, Wisconsin and now of Iron

Visit & RIDE
A REAL OLDTIME
STEAM TRAIN
ONE HOUR 13 MILE EXCURSIONS

Keweenaw Central Ry.
Steam Passenger Excursion Trains
Calumet, Mich.

ORIG. EST. 1906

THE COPPER COUNTRY ROUTE

UPPER MICHIGAN'S HISTORIC STEAM EXCURSION RAILWAY

------- NORMAL STEAM TRAIN OPERATING SCHEDULE: -------

WEEKENDS: ◆◆◆◆◆◆◆◆◆◆◆◆◆◆◆◆◆◆◆◆◆ STARTING MEMORIAL DAY

DAILY TRAINS: ◆◆◆◆◆◆◆◆◆◆◆◆◆◆◆◆◆◆◆◆◆ LATE JUNE THROUGH LABOR DAY WEEKEND

WEEKENDS: ◆◆◆◆◆◆ AFTER LABOR DAY WEEKEND. FALL COLOR TOURS INTO MID-OCTOBER

------- TRAIN DEPARTURES: -------

11:00 AM   1:30 PM   3:30 PM

DEPOT JUST OFF U.S. 41 VIA M-203 (MC LAIN PARK ROAD)

FARES & SCHEDULES SUBJECT TO CHANGE

River, Michigan; Vice-president and Treasurer Louis Keller, Cedar Rapids, Iowa; Vice-President Frank J. Glaisner, Glendale, Wisconsin; Vice-President Fred Tonne, a newspaperman, also of Glendale, Wisconsin; and Norman Fritz, an attorney of Waukesha, Wisconsin who was the secretary. Gerald J. Hinterberg was the master mechanic with Phil Dennis of Hancock and Bud Rowe of Centennial Heights as mechanics. Leonard Ollila, of Superior Location, was on the repair crew.

The Keweenaw Central Railway began steam train excursions on July 1, 1967, using ex-Copper Range engine Number 29, a fine-appearing unit. The tourist road had two other engines, a diesel Milwaukee Road unit and a Northwestern steamer. As for coaches, there were two small ones out of the Green Bay area and a large Soo line unit that formerly operated out of Minneapolis. A Burlington coach was also on hand. From the Copper Range Railroad, Coach

KEWEENAW CENTRAL RAILWAY
"THE COPPER COUNTRY ROUTE"

CALUMET   MICHIGAN

SPECIAL EXCURSION TICKET
GOOD FOR ONE ROUND T...
ADULT PASSAGE
OVER LINES OF THIS RAILWAY COMPANY WHEN OFFICIALLY
DATED AND STAMPED ON REVERSE.

Keweenaw Central Railroad Steam Train at Calumet, Michigan.

No. 60, which had operated between McKeever and Houghton·and on the now closed Lake Superior and Ishpeming route between Big Bay and Marquette, was already owned by this new organization.

The "Copper Country Route" designation and the three-topped copper ingot were adopted as the herald of the line, inasmuch as copper was the principal natural resource of the peninsula, and most of it in past years had been shipped out in ingot form. Thus, almost exactly sixty years from its original establishment as the Keweenaw Central Line, the line again offered steam passenger excursion trips in the area. The Copper Country Route carried summer excursionists over the scenic Trap Rock Valley rim to Lake Linden and return.

A high point of the thirteen mile "Copper Country Route" round trip tour was Bridge No. 30, spanning the Douglass Houghton Creek. The trestle became nationally famous as a result of the new operations, its visitors and the railways' promotional efforts for the entire area.

Bridge No. 30 was a 350 foot long all-steel trestle, rising on concrete piers 120 feet over Douglass Houghton Creek. As the train slowly crossed this spectacular trestle, one could view the top of the beautiful Douglass Houghton Falls in the tree-lined way to the rear of the canyon over which the

Steam locomotive is at the stand pipe at Calumet Junction taking on water. Clint Jones bought the Copper Range Railroad and this locomotive.

passenger rode. It could be reached off Highway M-26 if a person chose to drive there.

The old water standpipe was located at the Calumet Junction and here the locomotive took on water several times daily. Passengers could get off the train and watch the fireman or engineer pull down the huge spigot and fill the tender. When they swung the water pipe up and back, the train was ready to go again. Gregory Peet worked as the fireman during the summer of 1969, and remembers joking with onlookers during this water stop. Since the water spout was actually at the end of the Calumet city water main, this meant that the water was the same drinking water that residents received when they opened their tap in their houses in town. Since the water was perfectly safe for drinking, I would often catch some in a large-mouth applesauce jar to drink on the trip. The cab of a steam locomotive was naturally quite hot, and a swig of cold water was very refreshing.

Riders of the train would get off to watch this activity, and seeing me collecting water in such a way, they would often ask if I was collecting a water sample to see if it was OK to use in the boiler. "No, I would reply, "I'm just really thirsty." As I would then take a drink, often their eyes would become wide, thinking that I might be drinking some harmful contaminates instead of perfectly safe drinking water from the city of Calumet.

The train stopped just south of Bridge No. 30, then slowly backed over it again. The train then returned over the same tracks to the Calumet train yard.

Engine No. 29 was said to be the last steam engine in the Copper Country. It came out of a long hibernation from the Copper Range roundhouse, where it had been idle since 1953. It was officially retired in 1951, but enjoyed a brief return to serve when two of Copper Range Railroad's diesels were out of action. Now in June of 1967 it puffed and chugged as it tugged 450 tons into a new world and a new career. The big freight locomotive was engineered by Louis Keller. He piloted the burly power plant through a restricted area in the Copper Range yards in the vicinity of the roundhouse. The engine moved alone and no coupling to other cars took place. Purpose of the trials was to determine its ability to sustain protracted steam pressure. In this respect the test was highly important and revealed that old number 29 had an excellent constitution.

Delivering engine No. 29 and coach 60 to the Keweenaw Central property was a Copper Range Railroad diesel crewed by Edward Laurn, engineer; Carl Wuoti, fireman; Gus Kumlin and Karl Ponnikas, brakemen; and Cy LaBissoniere, conductor. Scores of local residents turned out to cheer the initial run, which carried Copper Range Railroad personnel William P. Nicholls, J. Roland Ackroyd, Charles Sincock, Edward Miller, Robert L. Mayworm, and Carl Bay as passengers.

Number 29 did not move between Houghton and Lake Linden under its own power but it did have approximately 180 pounds of steam it could use provided it had permission. It must be understood that the Copper Range officials abided by all rules, and, until the locomotive was turned over to its own tracks outside Lake Linden, it moved under the power of a Copper Range Railroad locomotive of the diesel type. As the train left the Houghton depot and continued along its path, the steam engine blew more warning whistles than did the diesel which ran ahead. According to President Jones, the trip was momentous and he was only too willing to give the passed folks an opportunity to realize that a steam locomotive again was functioning between Lake Linden and Calumet.

Once the train moved across M-26 north of Lake Linden the equipment was on its own. The Copper Range locomotive went back to Houghton performing its own business tasks. Several thousand persons were passed along the route and these appeared overjoyed at what they saw. Several hundred photos were taken and many cars followed the train from Houghton to Lake Linden and then to Calumet. Inasmuch as the Calumet depot is near Pine Street, additional hundreds

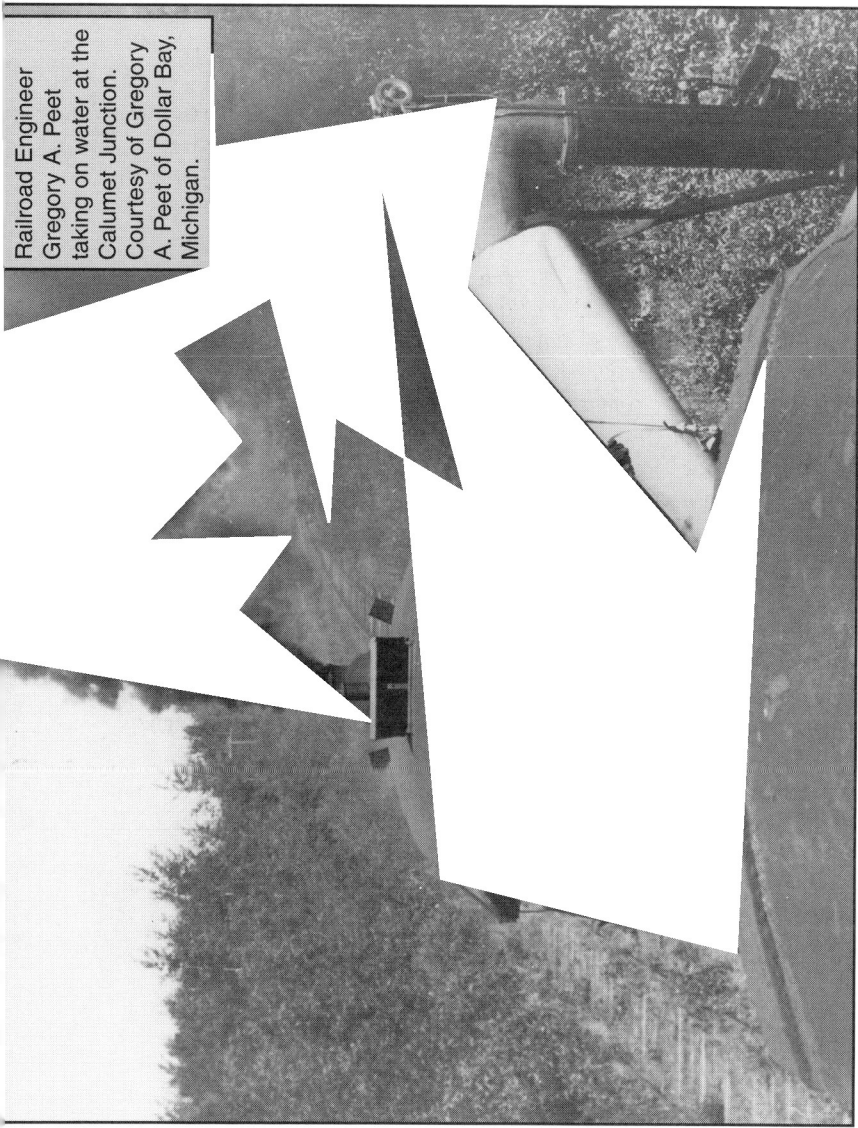

Railroad Engineer Gregory A. Peet taking on water at the Calumet Junction. Courtesy of Gregory A. Peet of Dollar Bay, Michigan.

appeared on the scene to witness Calumet's again possessing an oldtime steam railroad.

Before the train departed from Houghton, Fred Tonne, a Milwaukee newspaper man and part owner of the new route and its equipment gave a short talk to those assembled at the Houghton Copper Range depot. His words had to do with giving high appreciation to William Nicholls of the Copper Range Railroad for diligence he observed in saving No. 29 and one of the Copper Range coaches for the new route. Nicholls commented that he did not want No. 29 and the coach to get out of the Keweenaw Peninsula and that if ever the Keweenaw Central had no use for it, the option was the Houghton line's right to repurchase. Douglas Mechlin and the Calumet and Hecla Mining Company also came in for complimentary words. He paid tribute to the mining firm for its consideration of the new tourist line and for the permission given it to use certain trackage controlled by the copper mining concern.

Tonne lauded Joseph Lenz of the Houghton National Bank, which also came in for praise due to it being the Houghton institution which had facilitated the development of the route through financial aid. The 60 year old train would now run through a timber and mining region of Michigan's Upper Peninsula. Number 29 was built by the American Locomotive Company in 1907, delivered to the Copper Range

Railroad dock in Houghton, where it served until retirement in 1948. It was a 2-8-0 type, called a "Consolidation", weighing 135 tons in running order, carried nine tons of coal, 5,000 gallons of water, and 180 pounds working steam pressure. Its "extended wagon top" boiler was hand-fired. It had a license to operate at 180 pounds of steam pressure. Number 29 had eight 50-inch diameter drive wheels, and a unique, permanent attached snow plow on its pilot; perhaps the only such one still operating as a steam locomotive in the entire country.

It was appropriately decorated in a new paint job. New lettering was applied and the tender sported the name "Keweenaw Central Railroad." When engine 29's whistle was blown, ah, so nostalgic that many people in the area found it easy to recall the swishing sound of previous steamers which saw steam turn into vapor as the "white smoke" exuded from the areas about

other locomotive's drive shafts. It was authorized to travel with tourists between ten and fifteen miles per hour over the initial stages of the track.

The "Green Coach," formerly Burlington Route No. 6114, was a commuter style, long in service with that line. The "Yellow Coach," the last passenger coach in the Copper Country in regular service, was ex-Copper Range Railroad No. 60 which was built about the turn of the century. These were called "open vestibule" style. Coach 60 and Engine 29 were long preserved by the Copper Range in their Houghton Roundhouse, before being acquired by the Keweenaw Central Railway.

In 1968 the Company purchased a plush business car which formerly belonged to the Burlington Railroad. The Keweenaw Central purchased the car for its own clerical reasons but it was also decided that it would become an occasional car to move hither and yon in pursuit of the Keweenaw Central and other lines' desires. It was brought to Houghton by a double diesel unit Copper Range Railroad train and later pulled to Lake Linden where it was taken in tow by Copper Range's former engine, No. 29 which was now the property of the Keweenaw Central. Numbered 99, the car was steel with roller bearings and had six wheel trucks and was built in 1905.

Gregory A. Peet knocking soot from the smokebox of Keweenaw Central Railroad locomotive number 29 during the summer of 1969. Courtesy of the Gregory A. Peet collection.

This car was nicely equipped with rooms, executives' area with dining table, could sleep eleven persons; it also possessed appropriate lounge chairs, its own electrical outlets and one of those proper platforms so desired by businessmen in days gone by. Many a touring politician in those days spoke from such platforms on behalf of his candidacy or some other politician he was assisting.

Company President Clint Jones could easily give a lecture on this lush car because he had studied it from "stem to stern" and he well realized that its cost was $20,000 when it was new in 1905. It had gone through some improvements and was now one of the showpieces of the Copper Country.

A caboose was the sixth item of rolling stock. The intensely red tail end car was from the Iowa Central Railroad line, number 0833, was in good condition and would make a proper terminus car for the new train.

A second caboose was purchased in March of 1968 when it was switched from the Soo Line freight yard to the Copper Range yard. The caboose was No. 584 and was built in 1922 at its Shoreham, Minnesota, car shops. It weighed about 40,000 pounds and was ideally constructed for easy riding. This end car came in via the Soo Line from the Nestoria trackage link to which location it was transferred from Ashland, Wisconsin, where it had been serving on a varied Soo route. It was known that this caboose was a former Duluth South Shore and Atlantic caboose and it had traveled far and wide on runs between Milwaukee, Minneapolis, Sault Ste. Marie, Keweenaw Peninsula, and the Marquette region.

It was in good condition except for a broken glass or two. It would soon be repaired and become a Caboose Special. A Caboose Special was frequently enjoyed by those who admired riding tourist trains of the steam variety and the customer is permitted to climb the inside steps to the high, central roost where he has the privilege of observing the passing route just as one may do in some of the dome cars of the trancontinental lines.

On July 1, 1967, The Keweenaw Central Railroad had its trial run. The Keweenaw Central crew conisted of Clint Jones, engineer; Louis S. Keller, brakeman; Gerald Hinterberg, fireman; Fred Tonne, conductor; Fred Glaisner, brakeman; and Marty Anderson, helper. Douglas Mechlin, analyzer of the route and Calumet and Hecla Division railway official, aided in piloting the train on its run.

When the excursions started, Treasurer Lou Keller was the conductor who performed the narration work and also answered the clientele's questions. Lou said that passengers would only be permitted aboard in Calumet where facilities were ready for boarding.

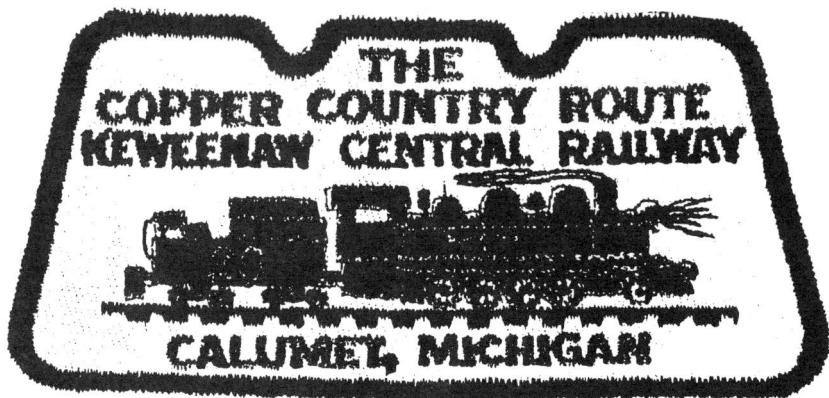

Gerald Hinterberg, the line's master mechanic, was the Keweenaw Central's fireman and it was he who observed steam gauges, boiler water contents and the general line as the train proceeded on its route. Old Number 29 consumed three-quarters of a ton of coal per hour and the steam pressure was maintained at 160 pounds since the locomotive was not forced to pull more than two coaches and a caboose. The tracks rose 375 feet in less than six miles.

The switching operation at Lake Linden to prepare for the return trip was unusual and very interesting. This was particularly memorable to Greg Peet, fireman during 1969, since each time he got to run the steam locomotive himself as part of the operation. There was a passing siding nearby, but it was just across highway M-26, and the train was not allowed to cross that state highway. Therefore extra

Upper Peninsula's Keweenaw Central Railway excursion train goes over Michigan's highest passenger bridge, a steel span 120 feet above Douglass Houghton Creek.

maneuvering was necesssary to get the engine on the front of the train for the return trip to Calumet.

Peet recalls, "The train stopped at the switch in to Silver Forest Products. I would throw the switch for the siding and uncouple the cars which were left on the main line. While engineer Clint Jones would run the engine into the siding, I would again line the switch for the main line. Clint would then start up an ex-Milwaukee Road Whitcomb 44-tonner diesel, advance uphill to the parked cars, couple on and pull them back south of the switch. Having stayed at the switch, I would next align it for the siding again, and then walk to No. 29, back it out onto the mainline, dismount, align the switch for the mainline once again, and then allow the engine to drift downhill to couple onto the passenger cars, but this time on the north or uphill end of the train, ready for the trip back."

In the meantime, Clint would have uncoupled the 44-tonner from the train and walked into position to signal to me regarding the coupling. As he connected the air brakes and walked back to the steam locomotive cab, I would be busy preparing the fire for the steep uphill trip back to Calumet. Although this sounds complicated, it only took a matter of minutes since it was orchestrated so well. Being done on every trip it became almost second nature. But moving the Johnson bar to

control direction and pulling the
throttle on the big 135 ton steam
locomotive never became second nature.
It was a thrill every time."

   In June of 1970, in an attempt to
create areawide cooperation among the
Copper Country organizations that were
striving to improve the local economic
and cultural climate, the Keweenaw
Central offered to provide a steam ride
for the Houghton County Historical
Museum's benefit. Clint Jones,

HOUGHTON COUNTY HISTORICAL SOCIETY

1961

MUSEUM BUILDING M-26
LAKE LINDEN, MICHIGAN

STEAM EXCURSION ABOARD THE
KEWEENAW CENTRAL RAILWAY
Calumet, Michigan, June 27, 1970
Saturday Evening 7:00 P.M.

Adults $2.00 — — — Children $1.00
(Good for one round trip)
(all proceeds for Historical Museum Benefit)

President of the Keweenaw Central made
this proposal to the museum's board of
directors and they warmly accepted. An
"Excursion with Steam" took place on
Sunday evening, June 27, 1970, leaving
from the Calumet depot, for a cost of
adults $2.00 and children $1.00.

During the spring of 1971 the
Keweenaw Central obtained an electric-
diesel locomotive. The engine M-35, a
65 foot long, 400 horsepower
diesel-electric Railway Post Office -
Baggage Motor Unit, Pullman-built in
1929 as a gas-electric unit costing
then nearly $50,000.00 was the last and
only survivor of a 75 engine fleet
which was on the consolidated
Burlington Northern lines, America's
largest, 25,859 mile railroad system.
On the Burlington it was Engine 9735.
Its gas engine was replaced by a
diesel-electric unit by the line in
1949.

Gas-electric, and later
diesel-electric units were frequently
unofficially called "Doodlebugs" by
both railroad men and passengers, and
scarcely a branch line in the Midwest
existed that at one time or another
didn't see them in regularly scheduled
short-run passenger trains.

Originally built for the Chicago,
Burlington and Quincy Railroad as
Engine 9735, it served with its sister
units on that line in light passenger,
freight, branch line and yard switching
service until 1966. The 9735 ended its
Burlington days as yard switcher in
Macomb, Illinois.

Number 9735 was sold to the
Southern Industrial Railway, of
Centerville, Iowa in 1966, where it
worked until the line ceased operations
in 1968. The engine stood idle in a

Courtesy of Gregory A. Peet
of Dollar Bay, Michigan.

county highway yard spur and scrap yard until spring of 1971, when the Keweenaw Central owners acquired it for preservation and regular re-operation early in the spring, shipped it North, and restored it to regular operation.

The new owners had the engine repainted orange, red and black, with red and white contrast stripes on its nose and rear, a color scheme similar to the Milwaukee Road's famed "Chippewa" passenger trains that once served the Lake Superior district of the Upper Peninsula. Excursion riders could now hear the tones of its newly installed five-chime whistle echoing over the Trap Rock Valley and the wooded gorge walls of Douglass Houghton Creek.

It was reported by the Daily Mining Gazette in July, 1971, that the Keweenaw Central had quite a unit of pioneer rolling stock right in their yard. They were as follows: Two Green Bay and Western combines; two Burlington coaches, one No. 60 Copper Range coach; one Soo Line caboose and another Milwaukee Railroad caboose; one business car; one Milwaukee Road box car; one Soo Line combine; one solarium; one flat car; one diesel-electric motorcar; one Copper Range steamer; one Chicago and Northwestern steamer and one Plymouth industrial engine of ten tons.

The line terminated operations in 1971 after it received national respect from thousands of visitor-riders and railroad buffs. It was forced to terminate when the Copper Range Railroad whose tracks went to Houghton, and joined the Keweenaw Central's tracks near the Lake Linden hill, announced its abandonment petition. This action would leave the Keweenaw Central totally isolated from all railroad connections and with no rails to join any other railroad lines.

Its "Grand Finale" was on Sunday, October 10, 1971, as a standing-room-only trainload of excursionists stood behind the last train. Some of the people on the last run were Attorney Richard Kedzior, counsel for the line; brakeman Edward A. Robinson, St. Paul Keweenaw Central accountant; Engineer and President Clinton Jones Jr.; and Charles Sincock, retired vice president of the Copper Range Railroad. "Last Run" passengers came from Milwaukee, Chicago, Duluth, St. Paul, Madison and Detroit.

It was announced on September 20, 1971 that the former route of the Keweenaw Central between Copper City and Calumet Junction was now witnessing its rails being removed. The route was three miles long. Most of the rails were of the sixty pound class and were placed on the site in 1906. The rail was shipped to Pennsylvania where it was rolled into shapes and various types angles. Some were being made into iron going into sign posts.

In October 1972 the contingent of locomotives, coaches, club cars, caboose, and business cars departed from Calumet on the Keweenaw Central Line for Lake Linden, pulled by the Central's motor car to the junction with the Copper Range near the top of Lake Linden Hill, which was next to Highway 26.

At Lake Linden, the unit of eight cars and three locomotives was taken in tow by a Copper Range locomotive and pulled to its first stop at Ripley, where the three engines were shunted in exchange rights by the Copper Range locomotive on the Soo Line to a covering in the mineral shed of the Quincy Mining Company at the smelter site.

A Copper Range locomotive pulled the eight cars to Houghton where they were delivered to McKeever, then turned over to the Milwaukee Road for transit to Channing where the Escanaba and Lake Superior Line took over and brought them to Escanaba for temporary storage.

After the rail cars left the area, the Keweenaw County Road Commission removed the tracks from U.S. 41 highway and repaved the road as it did with former crossings of the Calumet and Hecla Line. The tracks of the line between Calumet and Lake Linden were removed the next year, 1973.

It was announced on July 19, 1973 that the Trans Northern (Keweenaw Central) sold the old South Shore Line, Calumet railroad depot, which had been closed for several years, to a Detroit businessman, James Leinonen. The

depot, once headquarters of the
Calumet-based Mineral Range Railroad,
later became the passenger station for
the Duluth, South Shore and Atlantic,
which ultimately was merged into the
Soo Line, which last used the station.

The Keweenaw Central Railway had
purchased the station with a view
toward expansion of its excursion train
services, but when the Keweenaw Central
was forced to close, owners felt no
further need to keep the old depot.

SOURCES

The references listed below were used in gathering information to aid in the writing of this publication. Not all of the sources are listed however, as many people of the Copper Country provided much information.

I particularly used the resources of the Michigan Technological University Library and the Daily Mining Gazette, both located in Houghton. I am indebted to Verna K. Masters of the Michigan Technological University for her assistance from the Library Archives and Roy Paananen of Marquette for all the data, pictures and maps he provided.

PUBLICATIONS

Reports of the Keweenaw Copper Company for the years 1905 through 1942

Lac La Belle, by Clarence J. Monette, 1990

The Copper Handbook, by Horace J. Stevens, Vol. 5, 1915 through Vol. XI, 1912-1913

The Mines Handbook, by Walter Harvey Weed, E. M., Vol XII, 1916 through Vol. XVII, 1931.

Poor's Manual of Railroads, by Poor's Railroad Manual Company, 1910, page 831

Michigan Railroads and Railroad
  Companies, by Graydon M. Meints,
  1992

Copper Range News, Vol. 7, No. 8,
  August 1967 (Article: Old No. 29
  Still Rolls)

NEWSPAPERS

Portage Lake Mining Gazette, Houghton,
  Michigan

Sunday Mining Gazette, Houghton,
  Michigan

Daily Mining Gazette, Houghton,
  Michigan

The Mining Journal, Marquette, Michigan

The Calumet News, Calumet, Michigan

The Copper Country News, Calumet,
  Michigan

The Iron Ore, Ishpeming, Michigan

The Keweenaw Miner, Mohawk, Michigan

OTHER

Printed data, pictures and maps from
  the Roy Paananen of Marquette.
  Michigan collection

Data, pictures and memories from
Gregory A. Peet of Dollar Bay,
Michigan

Herman Page Collection, maintained at
the Library Archives, Michigan
Technological University, Account
No. 22

Vertical Files, Keweenaw Central
Railway Steam Train, Library
Archives, Michigan Technological
University, Houghton, Michigan

Vertical Files, Amusement, Crestview,
Library Archives, Michigan
Technological University, Houghton,
Michigan

University Term Paper, Keweenaw Central
Railroad, by Rich Calvin, 1986,
Michigan Technological University
call number HE 2791.K43.C3

ADD THIS COPPER COUNTRY LOCAL HISTORY
SERIES TO YOUR PERSONAL LIBRARY

COR-AGO, A LAKE LINDEN MEDICINE COMPANY
First of a local history series

A COPPER COUNTRY LOGGER'S TALE
Second of a local history series

GREGORYVILLE - THE HISTORY OF A HAMLET LOCATED ACROSS
FROM LAKE LINDEN, MICHIGAN
Third of a local history series

WHITE CITY - THE HISTORY OF AN EARLY COPPER COUNTRY
RECREATION AREA
Fourth of a local history series

SOME COPPER COUNTRY NAMES AND PLACES
Fifth of a local history series

THE HISTORY OF LAKE LINDEN, MICHIGAN
Sixth of a local history series

THE HISTORY OF JACOBSVILLE AND ITS SANDSTONE QUARRIES
Seventh of a local history series

THE HISTORY OF COPPER HARBOR, MICHIGAN
Eight of a local history series

THE HISTORY OF EAGLE HARBOR, MICHIGAN
Ninth of a local history series

LAKE LINDEN'S YESTERDAY - A PICTORIAL HISTORY, VOLUME I
Tenth of a local history series

THE HISTORY OF EAGLE RIVER, MICHIGAN
Eleventh of a local history series

JOSEPH BOSCH AND THE BOSCH BREWING COMPANY
Twelfth of a local history series

COPPER FALLS - JUST A MEMORY
   Thirteenth of a local history series

THE CALUMET THEATRE
   Fourteenth of a local history series

EARLY DAYS IN MOHAWK, MICHIGAN
   Fifteenth of a local history series

LAKE LINDEN'S YESTERDAY - A PICTORIAL HISTORY, VOLUME II
   Sixteenth of a local history series

THE KEWEENAW WATERWAY
   Seventeenth of a local history series

A BRIEF HISTORY OF AHMEEK, MICHIGAN
   Eighteenth of a local history series

ALL ABOUT MANDAN, MICHIGAN
   Nineteenth of a local history series

HANCOCK, MICHIGAN, REMEMBERED, VOLUME I
   Twentieth of a local history series

THE SETTLING OF COPPER CITY, MICHIGAN
   Twenty-first of a local history series

LAKE LINDEN'S YESTERDAY - A PICTORIAL HISTORY, VOLUME III
   Twenty-second of a local history series

PAINESDALE, MICHIGAN - OLD AND NEW
   Twenty-third of a local history series

SOME OF THE BEST FROM C & H NEWS - VIEWS, VOLUME I
   Twenty-fourth of a local history series

HANCOCK, MICHIGAN, REMEMBERED - CHURCHES OF HANCOCK,
VOLUME II
   Twenty-fifth of a local history series

OJIBWAY, MICHIGAN, A FORGOTTEN VILLAGE
   Twenty-sixth of a local history series

LAURIUM, MICHIGAN'S EARLY DAYS
Twenty-seventh of a local history series

DELAWARE, MICHIGAN, ITS HISTORY
Twenty-eight of a local history series

LAKE LINDEN'S LIVING HISTORY - 1985
Twenty-ninth of a local history series

SOME OF THE BEST FROM C & H NEWS - VIEWS, VOLUME II
Thirtieth of a local history series

THE GAY, MICHIGAN, STORY
Thirty-first of a local history series

EARLY RED JACKET AND CALUMET IN PICTURES, VOLUME I
Thirty-second of a local history series

LAKE LINDEN'S DISASTROUS FIRE OF 1887
Thirty-third of a local history series

PHOENIX, MICHIGAN'S HISTORY
Thirty-fourth of a local history series

FREDA, MICHIGAN, END OF THE ROAD
Thirty-fifth of a local history series

HOUGHTON IN PICTURES
Thirty-sixth of a local history series

THE COPPER RANGE RAILROAD
Thirty-seventh of a local history series

LAC LA BELLE
Thirty-eight of a local history series

TRIMOUNTAIN AND ITS COPPER MINES
Thirty-ninth of a local history series

EARLY RED JACKET AND CALUMET IN PICTURES, VOLUME II
Fortieth of a local history series

UPPER PENINSULA'S WOLVERINE
  Forty-first of a local history series

REDRIDGE AND ITS STEEL DAM
  Forty-second of a local history series

THE MINERAL RANGE RAILROAD
  Forty-third of a local history series

WINONA AND THE KING PHILIP PROPERTIES
  Forty-fourth of a local history series

ATLANTIC MINE: PHOTOGRAPHS FROM THE
HAROLD H. HEIKKINEN COLLECTION
  Forty-fifth of a local history series

SOME OF THE BEST FROM C & H NEWS - VIEWS, VOLUME III
  Forty-sixth of a local history series

ALLOUEZ, NEW ALLOUEZ AND BUMBLETOWN
  Forty-seventh of a local history series

SOME FATAL ACCIDENTS IN THE ATLANTIC, BALTIC,
CHAMPION, TRIMOUNTAIN AND WINONA COPPER MINES
  Forty-eighth of a local history series

EARLY SOUTH RANGE, MICHIGAN, VOLUME I
  Forty-ninth of a local history series

CENTRAL MINE: A GHOST TOWN
  Fiftieth of a local history series

BALTIC, MICHIGAN
  Fifty-first of a local history series

KEWEENAW CENTRAL RAILROAD AND THE CRESTVIEW
  RESORT
  Fifty-second of a local history series